Comparative Law for Legal Translators

NEW TRENDS IN TRANSLATION STUDIES

Volume 17

Series Editor:
Professor Jorge Díaz Cintas

Advisory Board:
Professor Susan Bassnett
Dr Lynne Bowker
Professor Frederic Chaume
Professor Aline Remael

PETER LANG

Oxford • Bern • Berlin • Bruxelles • Frankfurt am Main • New York • Wien

Comparative Law for Legal Translators

Guadalupe Soriano-Barabino

PETER LANG

Oxford • Bern • Berlin • Bruxelles • Frankfurt am Main • New York • Wien

Bibliographic information published by Die Deutsche Nationalbibliothek.
Die Deutsche Nationalbibliothek lists this publication in the Deutsche National-
bibliografie; detailed bibliographic data is available on the Internet at
http://dnb.d-nb.de.

A catalogue record for this book is available from the British Library.

Library of Congress Cataloging-in-Publication Data

Names: Soriano-Barabino, Guadalupe, 1973- author.
Title: Comparative law for legal translators / Guadalupe Soriano-Barabino.
Description: Oxford ; New York : Peter Lang, 2016. | Series: New trends in
  translation studies ; volume 17 | Includes bibliographical references and
  index.
Identifiers: LCCN 2016005557 | ISBN 9783034317252 (alk. paper)
Subjects: LCSH: Comparative law. | Law--Translating. |
  Translators--Handbooks, manuals, etc.
Classification: LCC K559 .S667 2016 | DDC 340/.2--dc23 LC record available at
http://lccn.loc.gov/2016005557

ISSN 1664-249X

ISBN 978-3-0343-1725-2 (print) • ISBN 978-1-78707-041-7 (ePub)
ISBN 978-1-78707-042-4 (mobi) • ISBN 978-1-78707-040-0 (ePDF)

© Peter Lang AG, International Academic Publishers, Bern 2016
Hochfeldstrasse 32, CH-3012 Bern, Switzerland
info@peterlang.com, www.peterlang.com, www.peterlang.net

This publication has been peer reviewed.

Printed in Germany

Contents

Figures

Tables

Acknowledgements

This volume is the logical consequence of over twenty years of study, teaching and research. As a law graduate and a translation graduate, I have had the chance to study the law of different countries and to apply my legal knowledge to the translation of legal texts, which has always given me great satisfaction and has allowed me to enjoy the secrets of legal translation, first as a student and later as a translator and a translator trainer. And as there is no path that can be walked alone; there are many people whom I have encountered in my journey through legal translation and whom I would like to thank for their support.

For the elaboration of this volume I must thank Angela Carpi, from the University of Bologna, for her contribution on Italian law. Likewise Rafael Adolfo Zambrana Kuhn, from the University of Granada, contributed with his knowledge on the German legal system. Catherine Way, from the University of Granada, has read and corrected the whole manuscript and without her inestimable help it would not have been possible to accomplish this task. I would also like to thank everyone at Peter Lang, particularly Dr Laurel Plapp, Commissioning Editor, and Jorge Díaz Cintas, Series Editor, as well as the readers of earlier versions of the manuscript, for their invaluable comments and suggestions.

For the day-to-day path followed to this finish line I have to thank, first of all, my family and, most especially, my parents, for always believing in me and for giving me the chance to fulfil my dreams. Secondly, my friends, for being always there. Thirdly, my colleagues, all of them, from my fellow student colleagues when, completely unaware, I commenced this adventure, to my colleagues at work, but most especially those who started as my teachers and became my friends, particularly Dorothy Kelly and Catherine Way, to whom I owe so much, the former as my guide all these years and the latter for showing me how to love the art of legal translation. Fourthly, Roberto Mayoral, for allowing me to learn from him. Fifthly, my students, for their patience and for what they have taught me. And last but not least, Antonio, Guillermo and Andrea, for their unconditional love and support and for the moments stolen, which I hope to be able to repay somehow someday.

Guadalupe Soriano-Barabino
Granada, May 2016

Introduction

The aim of this volume is not to explore legal translation as such but to offer an introduction to comparative law for translators of legal documents. It approaches comparative law from an applied perspective with a view to being a useful tool for translators-to-be, translator trainers and professional translators who wish to develop their activity in the field of legal translation.

The volume is divided into four broad parts, each one devoted to specific aspects of comparative law and its usefulness for translation. Even if some parts are more theoretical than practical, its relevance is justified by the need to acquire a certain subject area or thematic competence before tackling the translation of legal texts, as will be explained throughout the volume.

Part I of this volume puts comparative law and legal translation into perspective. Chapter 1 explores the meaning and development of comparative law and the relation between this discipline and translation. The reader will not find an exhaustive description of the meaning and scope of legal translation here, but rather an explanation of how and why comparative law can be a useful tool for the translation of legal texts.

Chapter 2 describes the legal families and traditions existing in the world, with special reference to the civil law family and the common law family, the two main Western traditions which are explained in this volume.

Part II of this volume is devoted to the civil law tradition. Several legal systems belonging to this family are described in the book and thus Chapter 3 is dedicated to Italy, Chapter 4 to France, Chapter 5 to Spain and Chapter 6 to Germany.

Part III is devoted to the other legal family described in this volume: the common law family. As in part two, several legal systems are described, specifically those of England and Wales in Chapter 7, the United States in Chapter 8 and Ireland in Chapter 9.

As will be explained further, legal systems are not analysed in depth, but only their main characteristics are outlined. In a volume such as this it would not be possible to describe the legal branches of all legal families. Besides, this is not our aim. Our intention is to offer a brief description of the main aspects of the legal systems described so that translators can then search for more detail according to their needs. We are convinced that in-depth analysis of branches, concepts, institutions, documents, etc. and their implications for translation are necessary to correctly translate between national laws and this volume intends to be a first step towards looking further into those aspects.

Part IV – the last part – aims to apply theory to practice. Theoretical knowledge of comparative law is of no use for translators if it cannot be applied to the practice of translation. In Chapter 10 we describe translation competence and analyse which are the primary areas of competence needed by translators of legal texts. This is followed by a discussion of what the ideal training for legal translators may be and, finally, a brief overview is offered of how legal translators are actually trained.

Chapter 11 offers a didactic approach to legal translator training from a comparative perspective. Translation techniques are explained and some examples on how to apply comparative law to legal translation practice are shown. Lastly, exercises for the training of translators of legal texts are suggested.

Finally, the bibliographical references referred to in this volume are presented.

PART I

Comparative Law and Legal Translation

This first part of the volume comprises two chapters. In Chapter 1 we define comparative law and analyse its development, nature, object of study and methodology to later study the interaction between comparative law and legal translation.

In Chapter 2 a brief overview of the main legal families of the world is offered, with special emphasis on the two legal families that gain prominence in this volume: the civil law and the common law families or traditions.

CHAPTER 1

Comparative Law and its Importance in Legal Translation

1.1 Definition of comparative law

The first step before studying the interaction between comparative law and legal translation would be to define what is meant by 'comparative law'. Comparative law is not a branch of law or of legal science, such as family law, administrative law or criminal law, among others, are. On the contrary, comparative law can be considered as a study and research methodology. Zweigert and Kötz (1998: 2) define it as 'an intellectual activity with law as its object and comparison as its process'. As the same authors point out, the extra dimension of comparative law is that of internationalism and this is what confers on this method of study its essence: comparative law is the comparison of the different legal systems of the world, not the comparison of different rules in a single legal system. The object of study of comparative law is, then, a plurality of legal systems and its aim is to confront them in order to analyse differences and similarities.

It is important to know that the mere study of foreign law is not comparative law as one only can speak of comparative law if there are specific comparisons of legal systems, legal institutions, legal problems, legal principles, legal rules, legal realities, and so on. That is, the description of every legal system, institution, problem, principle, rule or reality must be first laid out and then compared, so as to achieve the aim of the comparison.[1]

---

1   Some practical examples of how specific aspects of law can be compared and the application of such comparison for legal translation are shown in Chapter 11.

Likewise, it is not possible to talk about comparative law when the legal system we are 'comparing' or, rather, putting into perspective is just one legal system, even if it 'works' in different languages. Some examples of this would be that we cannot compare European Union law even if laws, regulations or directives can be found in different languages (as EU law is the same for all member states), nor can we compare the English and Irish versions of statutes enacted in Ireland, for instance, as they share a common legal system.

Hendry (2014) goes a step further when discussing the difference between comparative law and comparative legal studies. The former refers, according to this author, to 'the traditional, once mainstream, process of comparison' while the latter indicates 'those positivist approaches that are more sensitive to the importance of context' (*ibid.*: 88).

Brand (2009: 19) defines comparative law as 'the scholarly search for interrelations between different legal systems'. As Engberg (2013) points out, on the basis of this definition, comparative lawyers and translators share interests as all of them are attracted by the interrelation between legal systems, as will be analysed further in this volume.

Comparative law as a method of study was born in Paris in 1900 thanks to the celebration of an International Conference for Comparative Law. The early objectives of comparative law, according to Lambert (1905), were to resolve the accidental and divisive differences in the laws of peoples at similar stages of cultural and economic development, and to reduce the number of divergences in law, attributable not to the political, moral or social qualities of the different nations, but to historical accidents or to temporary or contingent circumstances. Today this method of study has evolved due to the development of the world itself and the following objectives of comparative law are currently prominent: (1) academic study, law reform and policy development, (2) providing a tool for research towards a universal theory of law, (3) offering a perspective for students, (4) helping the international practice of law, (5) contributing to international unification and harmonization – common core research, (6) acting as a gap filling device in law courts, and (7) and being an aid to world peace (Orücü 2002).

The importance of comparative law today is found in its essence. Rojas Ulloa (2009) underlines the following aspects as those that confer on comparative law its current importance:

- It is a fundamental element of the legal culture.
- It implies a profound sense of humanism.
- It is embedded with a sense of universality.
- It allows for a better understanding of foreign law.
- It helps to understand problems solved by other legal systems.
- It enhances the characteristics, excellences and differences of our own legal system (as it is put into perspective).
- It is a requirement of current times for academic training and information, for the legal profession, legal education and social relations.
- It allows us to become familiar with different legal systems: their structure and how they work.
- It is a consequence of the globalization of law.

In addition, comparative law becomes an essential part of interdisciplinary research and practice in a discipline such as (legal) translation, as will be analysed further.

1.2 Development of comparative law

As we have just mentioned, the origin of modern comparative law as a method of study dates back to 1900, when the first International Conference on Comparative Law was held in Paris. However the roots of comparative law can be found much earlier.

The *Laws* of Plato, where he compares the laws of the Greek city-states, are considered to be the first example of comparative law, followed by Aristotle, who examined the constitutions of 153 states (Zweigert and Kötz 1998: 49). In Rome, the first example of comparative law can be traced back to the XII Tables. In the later imperial period, Roman law claimed validity throughout the whole Roman Empire, but it is known today that the eastern provinces continued to apply their local laws. According to Hug (1932) and to Zweigert and Kötz (1998), there is one comparative attempt in this era, ca. third or fourth century AD, called the *Collatio legum Mosaicarum et Romanorum*, an exposition of Roman law set against the laws of Moses. This work, which shows the similarities and differences of the two legal systems mainly with respect to tort and criminal law, can be considered as one of the 'earliest known works on comparative law' (Zweigert and Kötz 1998: 1033).

According to Hug (*ibid.*: 1034–5), after the fall of the West Roman Empire, Roman law was codified under Justinian in the East Roman Empire. In the western part of Europe individuals were subject to the law of their nation or tribe so that both Roman and Germanic laws were applied in the same territories, although this did not result in the creation of a common law nor of comparative studies, probably due to the modest scope of learning at that time (*ibid.*: 1035).

During the Middle Ages learning was revived, mainly thanks to Canon law,[2] but there was also a rise in secular scientific study and several schools devoted to the study of law were born, such as the Lombard School, which focussed on the study of feudal law, Canon law and Roman law and which, even though it did not create a scientific study of comparative law, could be said to have extended their knowledge to all the major legal systems of their time. The Glossators, the Commentators and the Bologna School followed the Lombard School and focused their efforts on studying Canon and Roman law. In England two works were published, where English and French law were compared, *De Laudibus Legum Angliae* and *The Governance of England* (Fortescue) but their aim was not so much to compare the law in these two countries, but to show the superiority of English law (Zweigert and Kötz 1998: 50).

---

2   A body of Roman ecclesiastical jurisprudence compiled in the twelfth, thirteenth and fourteenth centuries from the opinion of the ancient Latin fathers, the decrees of the General Councils, and the decretal epistles and bulls of the Holy See (Black 1991: 206).

More serious attempts at comparing various legal systems were made during the Renaissance. In France and Germany national legal scholars studied and compared customary law and, in other European countries, Roman and Germanic laws were compared, in some cases with reference to their own national laws, as is the case of the *Siete Partidas* in Spain; a statutory code first compiled under the reign of Alfonso X of Castile (1252–1284) with the aim of establishing a uniform body of normative rules for the country.

According to Hug (1932: 1045), the Reformation 'and the rising Law-of-Nature School with its aim at uniformity and its method of speculative rationalism did not promote empirical studies in comparative law'. On the contrary, the majority of the scholars of this school 'found the principles of their system of law by mere deduction and, though they did not consider any other system, they relied unconsciously upon the system of law with which they were most familiar' (*ibid.*). The study of comparative law was an exceptional occurrence and undertaken only by some (prominent) scholars such as Montesquieu, Vico, Grotius or Selden.

The first half of the nineteenth century can be considered to be the dawn of comparative law studies on a larger scale. Even if the unification and simplification of law in the European continent, which led to the codification in countries such as France or Germany, underlined the need for a practical legal science and studies in comparative law were seen as having no value, interest in foreign and comparative law was growing in these countries. In England, towards the middle of the nineteenth century, comparative law developed considerably due to two facts. On the one hand, the highest appellate court of the British Empire, the Privy Council, had to administer foreign legal systems because of the colonies under its control and, on the other hand, the international trade of English merchants made lawyers take an interest in understanding and accessing commercial laws of other countries. The legal experience of other countries was used on occasions to improve domestic law. As Hug (*ibid.*: 1069) points out, comparative law at this time was not to be discussed:

> as to the objects of such studies and the methods to be followed, but it developed a method of empirical observation and practical application of the results thus obtained

and was imbued with a keen and lasting interest, which may be regarded as a standard, even in our time, comparative law was, so to speak, still in embryo.

The twentieth century represents a shift in trends for comparative law. Up to this moment, comparative law was focussed on comparing legislation (in the broader sense of the term), but no method of study or science was developed. After the celebration of the 1900 Paris Conference, and due to some historical events (mainly, the two World Wars), comparative law started to interest scholars and some institutes devoted to the study of comparative law were created: the Institute for Comparative Law was founded in the University of Munich in 1916, whilst the Kaiser-Wilhelm Institute of Foreign and International Private Law and the Institute for Public Law, Foreign and International Law were founded in Berlin in 1926 (the latter now named *Max-Planck-Institut für ausländiches und internationales Privatrecht* and located in Hamburg). In France, 1920 saw the birth of the *Institut de Droit Comparé* in Lyons, followed by the *Institut de Droit Comparé* of Paris University, founded in 1932. Other international institutions created at this time are the *Académie Internationale de Droit Comparé*, founded in 1924 and the *Institut International pour l'Unification du Droit Privé* (UNIDROIT), created in Rome in 1926 by the League of Nations (Zweigert and Kötz 1998: 61). This rebirth of comparative law came with a shift of focus and the aim of this new method of study was now to compare the legal solutions 'given to the same actual problems by the legal systems of different countries seen as a complete whole' (*ibid.*), including all legal systems, not only comparable ones, as it was found useful to compare systems which were entirely different. This helped set the basis of a methodological approach to comparative law. In a similar vein, Dorbeck-Jung (1995) stressed the need for conceptualization of comparative legal studies as one of the challenges for law at the end of the twentieth century.

The history of comparative law in the twentieth century is summarized by the Call for Papers of the W. G. Hart Legal Workshop, held at the Institute of Advanced Legal Studies of the University of London on 4–6 July 2000:

Although for most of the 20th Century it appeared as if the ambitious project of legal unification set out in Paris was retreating from view as the world was torn apart by deep ideological conflicts, the last few years have seen a remarkable turnaround. Not only did the principal object of European legal unification make very significant advances from 1972: global economic and political conditions after the end of the Cold War (1945–89) made comparative law more immediately important and more worthwhile globally. The 1990s saw many positive developments in legal science and legal reform on every continent and advances in international norms. (Harding and Örücü 2002: vii–viii)

Nowadays, comparative law seems to have taken new directions, due mainly to the changes that have taken place in the socio-legal conditions in the world. As stressed by Goff (1997: 747–8), 'comparative law may have been the hobby of yesterday but is destined to become the science of tomorrow'.

In this regard, some of the concerns of comparative law today, as expressed by Bermann et al. (2011), are related to the criticisms received during the first decade of the twenty-first century – excessive doctrinalism, shuttered attitudes to interdisciplinary inquiry, timidity in approaching broad-gauge study, tendencies to superficiality, triviality, obscurantism, and exoticization – as well as to its incommensurability and its uneasy relationship with its sister disciplines, public and private international law. The main challenge of today's comparative law, according to these authors, would be 'to continue to make its intellectual curiosity, as well as its genuine appreciation of ideas, prevail over its undeniable practical utility' (*ibid.*: 940). Thus comparative law has also been criticized as been extremely instrumental and the challenge for the future would be to use the 'skills and knowledge of comparative lawyers in adding a normative dimension to the debate about comparative law' (*ibid.*: 943).

To these challenges we may add the current project to codify private law in the European Union, which will certainly involve not only an exercise of comparative law but also, and without any doubt, the interaction of legal translation.

1.3 The legal nature of comparative law

So far we have been referring to comparative law as a science or as a method of study. This is due to the fact that the different authors who study comparative law have not reached an agreement regarding its legal nature. Lambert (1905), one of the fathers of the discipline when it was born at the beginning of the twentieth century, considered it a science, as it has its own object of study (comparison of legal systems), final aim (contrasting legal systems and analysing differences and similarities) and configuration. Other scholars such as Gutteridge (1949) or David and Brierley (1985) consider it a method of study that can be used to understand and to further the knowledge of legal sciences. Comparative law has also been considered an accessory discipline (García Maynez 2002) to other legal sciences such as Jurisprudence or Legal Sociology. Similarly, it has been understood as an aid to law-making (Dorbeck-Jung 1995).

Despite all these debates, some authors, such as Örücü (2002), insist on the fact that there is still no agreement as to what comparative law and comparative method is today, or whether it is an independent discipline at all. More recently, Bermann et al. (2011) also stress the indeterminate nature of comparative law, regarded by many as a utilitarian doctrine where only its instrumental use is taken into account. These authors, however, defend the perception of comparative law as a means to an end, aiming at resolving concrete practical problems.

From what has been discussed so far we will bear in mind that comparative law has two main facets. On the one hand, it is embedded with a purely scientific aspect, being thus considered as a science or as a study and research discipline in itself. On the other hand, comparative law also has a practical side and in this sense, it is both a study method and an accessory discipline.

Furthermore, comparative law has two main perspectives: it can be descriptive, that is, it can be used to describe how legal systems or particular legal institutions within a legal system work, or it can be applied, in which case it is used as a tool to achieve other means. As will be analysed in the following pages, the usefulness of comparative law for legal translation lies precisely in this applied perspective of the discipline.

1.4 The object of study of comparative law

It goes without saying that the main aim of comparative law, as of any other science, is to further knowledge. From a philosophical and theoretical point of view, and taking into account the spirit that led the promoters of comparative law to consider it a method of study, it is said that it dissolves unconsidered national prejudices and it helps both to fathom the different societies and cultures of the world and to further international understanding. Therefore, this discipline can be useful for law reform in developing countries and for the development of one's own system (Zweigert and Kötz 1998). In this sense, it is generally assumed that the object of study of comparative law consists of confronting and comparing the legal systems and legal institutions existing in the world in order to analyse similarities and dissimilarities in their structure, as well as the reasons for them. The ultimate goal for this confrontation and comparison would be to promote and ensure the development of national law.

From a more practical perspective, authors such as Zweigert and Kötz (*ibid.*) have found four benefits of comparative law: (1) as an aid to the legislator; (2) as a tool for construction (interpretation of national rules of law); (3) as a component of the curriculum at universities, and (4) as a contribution to the systematic unification of law and the development of a private law common to the whole of Europe.

Other authors, like Rojas Ulloa (2009), set out several objectives of comparison, all leading to the aforementioned aim of promoting and assuring the development of national law:

- To have a better grasp of national law.
- To create an international legal language.

- To unify or harmonize legal systems.
- To have a better grasp of all legal systems.

These objectives and the reasoning behind them are particularly interesting for our aim. As Rojas Ulloa (2009) states, the act of comparing implies contrasting different legal systems and that can only be properly done when we master the language used by that particular legal system, which allows us to discover the exact meaning and nuances of the terminology used. This is why comparative law and (legal) language/translation interact in such a way that it is not possible to understand the one without the other: it is necessary to master the language to understand the texts of a particular legal system and it is necessary to understand the law in order to be able to translate that legal system into a different language.

The nature of the object of study of comparative law has been criticized for two main reasons. First of all, comparative law as such, what some authors call 'true' comparative law (Simonnaes 2013: 148) is quite rare as a national perspective is usually applied when comparing legal systems. Indeed, as argued by Merryman et al. (1994: 1, in Simonnaes, 2013: 148), the study of comparative law is often limited to the description of foreign legal systems. Secondly, the study of comparative law is often done from an ethnocentric, and Eurocentric (Örücü and Nelken 2007), point of view.

In this book, we do not study comparative law as a means in itself, but we use comparative law as a tool for training and practice in the field of legal translation. The final aim of the comparison is not to present its results but to produce a quality target text that suits a particular communicative situation. In this sense, numerous authors have stressed the importance and usefulness of comparative law for legal translation, including Biel and Engberg (2013), Dullion (2015), Glanert (2011, 2014), Lavoie (2013), Pommer (2008), Prieto Ramos (2009), Simonnaes (2013) and Soriano-Barabino (2002a, 2002b, 2005, 2013).

1.5 Comparative methodology

Even if the applied side of comparative law, particularly for legal translation, has developed considerably at the end of the twentieth century and
the beginning of the twenty-first century, from a strictly legal point of view
there has been little systematic research about the methodology used. This
is due to the fact that, even if comparative law has existed for a long time,
it is such a recent discipline that methodological principles have not been
fully developed (Zweigert and Kötz 1998: 33). In practice, the methodology
used in comparative law is close to that of the Social Sciences, placing legal
science on a realistic basis and relating it to the demands of real life. From
this perspective, the Social Sciences paradigm can therefore be considered to
be functional and appropriate for the study of comparative law (*ibid.*: 34).

The only 'rules' for comparison, from a methodological point of view,
are to establish the hypothesis (as in any other science) and to focus not on
the concept, but on the problem. This is explained by Zweigert and Kötz
(*ibid.*: 34) in the following terms: 'instead of asking, 'How does foreign
law regulate Vorerbschaft and Nacherbschaft?' one should try to find out
how the foreign law sets about satisfying the wish of a testator to control
his estate long after his death'; a piece of advice that is also equally valid
for translators. If we refer to traditional dictionaries that offer translation
solutions to terms, usually without any context or reference to the legal
culture of origin, the resulting translation will probably lack quality and
coherence and will surely not comply with the expectations of the reader.

The methodology recommended by comparatists would be the following: once we have focussed on a specific problem, the next step would
be to describe the solutions adopted by the legal systems to be compared,
then juxtapose them and finally compare the solutions given by each legal
system to that particular problem, so as to critically evaluate them. When
applied to the translation of legal texts, the 'problem' may be a concept,
an institution, a rule, a proceeding, a text (or a set of texts conforming, for
instance, a legal proceeding) for example.

Comparatists recommend contrasting the same realities in as many legal
systems as possible (mainly within the same legal family), and discourage

scholars from attempting to look at 'incomparables', as these cannot usually be compared. For some authors such as Zweigert and Kötz (*ibid.*: 34), the only aspects that are comparable in law 'are those which fulfil the same function' in the different systems; incomparables being realities that do not fulfil the same function. In the opinion of these authors, the basic methodological principle of all comparative law would be that of functionality. In the same vein, Simonnaes (2013: 147) asserts that 'to compare two objects or concepts generally presupposes that they are similar with respect to at least one aspect ("*tertium comparationis*")'. This author recognizes that the way in which similar objects or concepts are to be compared would depend partly on an objective criterion –the properties of the objects or concepts being compared– and partly on a subjective principle –what the person who is comparing considers is relevant for the comparison. Nonetheless, the same author is aware of the fact that in comparative law there is no unanimous understanding of what can be considered as *tertium comparationis*.

When this principle is applied to the translation of legal texts the assumption must be nuanced. The aim of translators when comparing legal realities is not to solve a particular problem, but rather to find the best way to translate a term or an expression and to be able to decide on how best to apply textual conventions in the target text with the overall aim of allowing the reader to understand the message that is being conveyed. Translators will work only with the legal systems to which the text/s they are translating belong, and they do not usually need to analyse other legal systems, although it may be useful in some circumstances, when equivalents do not exist or are not easily found, as a means to understand legal concepts or institutions from their source and target legal systems.

In addition, translators may on occasion need to compare 'incomparable' terms, expressions, institutions or (aspects of) legal systems belonging to different legal traditions. This is the case when a particular institution or concept may exist in one of the legal cultures but not in another, or when we may be working with legal systems as distant as a Muslim legal system and one belonging to the common law, for instance. The task of the translators necessarily calls for the comparison of terms, expressions, institutions and even whole legal systems that could be seen as totally divergent and impossible to compare. Translators need to find the translation for a certain institution, term, legal reality or document as part of a proceeding, or to find that a particular institution, term, legal reality or document in the other legal system does not have a 'comparable partner' and, in these cases, other ways must be found to come up with a suitable translation solution. From a translation perspective, the assertion that 'incomparables' cannot be compared does not hold.

It is also interesting to determine the extent to which the comparison can be made. Comparison has been traditionally assigned to comparative lawyers and understood as a quest of similarities and differences between the legal systems of different nations. Bearing this in mind, comparison can be done on a large or on a smaller scale. Comparing the spirit and style of different legal systems or the methods of thought and procedures they use has been termed 'macro-comparison'[3] (Zweigert and Kötz 1998: 4; Pizzorusso, 1987: 88), whilst the concept of 'micro-comparison' refers to 'specific legal institutions or problems, that is, with the rules used to solve actual problems or particular conflicts of interests' (Zweigert and Kötz 1998: 5).

Pizzorusso (1987: 88–9) states that the macro-comparison is usually done as a first step towards understanding the legal reality of the different legal systems whilst the micro-comparison requires a higher level of detailed study. We totally agree with this author and consider that this is also true for the translation of legal texts and, therefore, translators need a first general overview of the legal systems they work with in order to later analyse the specific branches, concepts and institutions therein. The usefulness and the application of these different methods of macro and micro-comparison for the translation of legal texts will be analysed in Chapter 11.

---

3   According to Zweigert and Kötz (1998: 4), when performing macro-comparison, 'instead of concentrating on individual concrete problems and their solutions, research is done into methods of handling legal materials, procedures for resolving and deciding disputes, or the roles of those engaged in the law. For example, one can compare different techniques of legislation, styles of codification, and methods of statutory interpretation, and discuss the authority of precedents, the contribution made by academics to the development of law, and the diverse styles of judicial opinion'.

1.6 Comparative law and legal translation

During the final decades of the past century, translation theory evolved
from a linguistic to a cultural approach. This means that translation is no
longer seen – as may have been the case before – as an activity involving
transferring words from one language to another, but rather about transferring ideas from one culture to another (Hönig and Kussmaul 1982; Vermeer
1986). As language is not an isolated phenomenon but an inseparable part
of any culture, cultural competence in translation becomes then as important as linguistic competence. Furthermore, as Snell-Hornby (1988: 44)
states, 'the translator must take account of the communicative function
of the target text and the elements constituting the sociocultural situation
in which it is produced'. This is also stressed by Pommer (2008: 17) who
expresses that 'since the Cultural Turn in Translation Studies, translation
is viewed as a cultural transfer, strategies to render possible an effective
communication between cultures'.

Our professional scenario is that of translating between legal systems,
rather than translating within a single multilingual structure or community.
Accordingly, it is important to bear in mind that law is a regional phenomenon and, in Pommer's (*ibid.*) own words, 'the roles of legal institutions
cannot be fully comprehended if not seen as part of their culture and at the
same time a culture cannot be fully understood without attending to its
form of law'. Consequently, legal language is the result of the history and
culture of a given country or region. This explains why each legal system
has its own legal language which is different from other legal languages. On
occasions, different legal systems may share the same or similar language,
but that does not mean that the legal reality is also shared. On this point,
Šarčević (1997: 67–8) states that:

> When dealing with legal texts, it is always necessary to determine according to which
> legal system the texts, parts thereof, or even individual institutions and concepts are
> to be interpreted. [...] the legal system according to which a text or parts thereof are
> to be interpreted is usually not determined by language.

In addition, legal terminology, as pointed out by Pommer (2008: 18) is 'system-bound, tied to the legal system' and therefore 'multiple legal languages can exist within the boundaries of a natural language, depending on how many legal orders make use of that same language'. To this it must be added that several different legal systems may coexist in one single country or region, as is the case in Canada, Hong Kong or the United States, to name just a few examples.

Due to this incongruence of legal systems, comparative law plays an important role in the translation of legal texts because, as has been explained above, it allows for the identification of similarities and dissimilarities between different legal systems. As underlined by Pommer (*ibid.*: 18), 'legal translators, as mediators between legal cultures have the task of effectively communicating legal information across the barriers of legal traditions and languages. In this pursuit, their major goal has to be to avoid conceptual misunderstandings and achieve transparency'. However, comparing legal systems (or concepts, institutions, text genres and the like) is not the same as translating and the comparison is not an end in itself for the translator, as explained in Section 1.4 above. The usefulness of comparative law for legal translation arises from its applied perspective as a tool for translators of legal texts. In this sense, legal translation becomes an exercise of comparative law. When translating legal texts, translators are faced with numerous challenges, including 'the asymmetry of legal systems, the relativity of legal terminology, inconsistent categorizations and classifications between the different branches and fields of law, distinguishing between the terminological and conceptual levels as well as the complexities of conceptual and terminological change' (*ibid.*: 18), and these challenges may be overcome thanks to the analysis of comparative law as a first step towards effective communication. The comparative analysis in the search for the best equivalents for the translation may result in a detailed comparison of legal realities and hence comparative law and legal translation interact in such a way that the former becomes an instrument of the latter and the latter is transformed into an analysis of the former. In this sense, Terral (2002: 4) states that this cultural dimension of legal translation is close to an exercise of comparative law as it is impossible to transfer a legal text from one legal system to another without mastering the legal cultures involved in this process. And, on the same topic, David and Brierley (1985: 16) underline the fact that:

> The absence of an exact correspondence between legal concepts and categories in different legal systems is one of the greatest difficulties encountered in comparative legal analysis. It is of course to be expected that one will meet rules with different content; but it may be disconcerting to discover that in some foreign law there is not even that system for classifying the rules with which we are familiar. But the reality must be faced that legal science has developed independently within each legal family, and that those categories and concepts which appear so elementary, so much a part of the natural order of things, to a jurist of one family may be wholly strange to another. This is true even as between those trained in a continental law and the common law, without going so far as to invoke Muslim law. Some matter of primary importance to one may mean nothing, or have only limited significance, to another. A question put by a European jurist, for example, to an African on a matter of family organisation or land law may well be totally incomprehensible if put to him in terms of European institutions.

This incongruence between legal systems has led several authors to describe it as the main challenge to the legal translator (Šarčević 1997). Therefore, the importance of being familiar with, or at least having the foundations, to know how to approach different legal systems is undoubtedly of utmost importance in legal translation training, as highlighted by Pelage (2001: 25, my translation):

> Relating two legal systems is indeed a problem for translators, as it is for lawyers. This fact leads us to compare legal systems not to other social systems, but to scientific systems.
>
> A mathematician, a physicist, a chemist, who have studied their discipline in the United States and have learnt to solve problems in a certain way, will be able to solve the same problems in Japan or in Sweden. That is, their technical knowledge is directly transferable to another environment. On the contrary, a lawyer specialized in inheritance law in French law will not be able to offer advice on an inheritance question in Spanish law, even if s/he speaks Spanish, unless s/he has studied both legal systems: his/her technical knowledge is not directly transferable to another legal context. This is a direct consequence of the basic relation between law and society.

Therefore legal translators become 'mediators' between legal systems and not only between languages (Prieto Ramos 2009). The practice of legal translation is one of the best examples of interdisciplinarity. This aspect is also underlined by Prieto Ramos (*ibid.*), who points out that it is in this discipline where the linguistic and the legal dimensions interact so as to create translation methods specifically for legal translators. This is seen by some authors, for example Dullion (2015), as contributing to its difficulty but also to its interest, as it differentiates it from other types of specialized translation such as the translation of technical texts.

To sum up, comparative law and legal translation interact because the former becomes an instrument for the latter. The asymmetry between different legal concepts and systems is a challenge for the translator and comparative law can help translators first to understand and later to explain (and translate) the legal concepts of the source legal system into the target legal system. The actual translation (as a product) can be rendered through the application of different techniques and strategies, which are discussed in detail in Chapter 11.

Translators should therefore be familiar with the legal systems with which they are working and must have the cultural and thematic or subject area competences necessary to be able to understand a concept, institution, rule, principle or document from a particular legal system and translate it into another legal system.[4] This is also stressed by Prieto Ramos (2011: 13), who asserts that

> even if legal translators do not need to be equipped with a jurist's level of legal expertise, it is essential that they acquire sufficient legal knowledge in order to situate the documents in their legal and procedural context, as well as to grasp the legal effects of original and target texts. In fact, legal translation between national systems normally entails an exercise of comparative law before any translation procedure can be applied to culturally-marked segments on reasoned grounds.

Sometimes the translation of these concepts will not involve the use of equivalent concepts, institutions, rules, principles or documents, possibly because these do not exist at all in the target culture or possibly because they do partially exist, but their meaning and function are not what the

---

4   For an explanation of the concept of translation competence and its different components see Chapter 10.

particular communicative situation of the target text requires. In these cases, other strategies and techniques should be put into place, but first we must know whether our referent exists in the target legal system, that is, we must start our translation process by undertaking an exercise of comparative law.

With this in mind, in the coming chapters (Chapters 2 to 9) the basic fundamentals are established for acquiring cultural and thematic or subject area competences. It is not our intention to fully explain all the legal systems of the world, not even the ones covered in this volume, but to offer translators some basic tools to tackle the translation of legal texts belonging to particular legal systems. At this point, it would be interesting to ask ourselves what kind of knowledge and how much comparative law is needed by translators. Of course, the legal knowledge translators need differs from that needed by lawyers, as the latter need to know the specific regulations, concepts and institutions so that they can apply the law to a particular case, whilst the former need to have a conceptual understanding of the same regulations, concepts and institutions, not with the aim of applying the law to a particular case, but to finding equivalents (or not) in another legal system, no matter whether we refer to concepts, rules, principles, documents, texts, proceedings or institutions. As for the second part of the question, as will be further analysed in Chapter 10, we are of the opinion that professional translators must have a comprehensive knowledge of the legal cultures involved in the translation process. Nonetheless, we acknowledge that such expertise is not possible at earlier stages of training or practice but we consider that the minimum amount of knowledge needed lies in a thorough understanding of how legal systems have originated and evolved, their organization and sources of law and the main elements interacting in the legal process. This has been our guiding principle when deciding how much (comparative) law to include in this volume.

CHAPTER 2

Legal Families and Traditions

In this chapter a brief overview of the main legal traditions of the world
is first offered to later focus on the civil law family and the common law
tradition.

2.1 The main legal families and traditions of the world

There have been several attempts to divide the existing legal systems of
the world into large groups, families or traditions 'in a taxonomic attempt
whose aim is to arrange the mass of legal systems in comprehensible order'
(Zweigert and Kötz 1998: 64). The difference between a 'legal family' or
'tradition' and a 'legal system' is that the former are 'not a set of rules of law
about contracts, corporations and crimes [...] rather a set of deeply rooted
historically conditioned attitudes about the nature of law, the role of law
in the society and the political ideology, the organization and operation of
a legal system and about the way law is or should be made, applied, studied, perfected and taught', whilst a legal system is 'an operating set of legal
institutions, procedures and rules' (Merryman 1985: 2). It can thus be said
that 'a legal tradition puts the legal system into cultural perspective', as it
'relates the legal system to the culture of which it is a partial expression'
(*ibid.*: 1). According to De Cruz (2007), legal systems are grouped under
a 'parent' legal family, such as the civil law family, or a 'major' legal system,
such as the common law system, thus creating legal families or traditions.
Legal families or traditions are 'group jurisdictions that may be classified
under a generic heading by virtue of having similar characteristics' (*ibid.*: 3).

David and Brierley (1985: 19) describe a legal system as a system which:

> has a vocabulary used to express concepts, its rules are arranged into categories, it
> has techniques for expressing rules and interpreting them, it is linked to a view of the
> social order itself which determines the way in which the law is applied and shapes
> the very function of law in that society.

Although the difference between a legal family or tradition and a legal
system seems rather straightforward, not all comparatists agree as to
which criteria should be taken into account when classifying legal systems
and allocating them to different legal families. Some of the attempts to
devise groupings of legal systems into families are those carried out by
Esmein (1905), Arminjon et al. (1950), David (1985) and Zweigert and
Kötz (1998).

Esmein (1905: 445), one of the pioneers in the field, divided the
legal traditions of the world into five families: Romanistic, Germanic,
Anglo-Saxon, Slav and Islamic. Some years later, Arminjon et al. (1950:
64) identified seven legal families according to their substance, 'paying due
heed to originality, derivation and common elements': French, German,
Scandinavian, English, Russian, Islamic and Hindu. David (1950) identified two main criteria for distinguishing legal systems and grouping them
into families: ideology (the product of religion, philosophy, or political, economic or social structure) and legal technique. On this basis, he
identified five different legal families: Western systems, socialist systems,
Islamic law, Hindu law and Chinese law. He later reduced his classification to only three families: the Romanistic-German family, the common
law family and the socialist family, along with a group of what he calls
'other systems' (not families at such), in which he includes Jewish law,
Hindu law the law of the Far East and a group of African and Malagasy
laws (David 1985).

Zweigert and Kötz (1998) criticize the divisions traditionally made
for various reasons. First, these authors defend that comparatists have
concentrated mainly on private law, and groupings may be relative as 'it is
quite possible that one legal system is to be put in one family for private
law purposes and in another for purposes of constitutional law':

> Arabian countries belong to Islamic law as far as family and inheritance law is concerned, just as India belongs to Hindu law, but the economic law of these countries [...] is heavily impressed by the legal thinking of the colonial and mandatory powers – the Common law in the case of India, French law in the case of most of the Arab states. (*ibid.*: 66)

Other aspects, such as the historical period in which the system is situated, must also be taken into account. For instance, the legal system of Japan has traditionally been classified, along with that of the People's Republic of China, as a Far-Eastern legal family; however the current legal system in Japan, highly influenced by the legal style dominant in the European continent, is closer to the civil law legal family than to the Far-Eastern one. In addition, new legal families may appear as different societies evolve (*ibid.*: 66).

The third aspect pointed out by these authors is that instead of basing categorizations on historical development, legal content or technique, more attention should be paid to whether different countries have the same legal culture and to whether their citizens have similar attitudes to the law and similar expectations. Hence, in their classification, they resort to legal style as the basis for grouping legal systems and they justify the use of this parameter because it has been used in other disciplines such as Law and Economics to indicate 'congeries of particular features which the most diverse objects of study may possess' (*ibid.*: 66). The factors they found crucial for the categorization of a legal system or family are as follows:

1. its historical background and development,
2. its predominant and characteristic mode of thought in legal matters,
3. its inclusion of especially distinctive institutions,
4. the legal sources it acknowledges and the way it handles them, and
5. its ideology. (*ibid.*: 68)

As a result, the authors group the existing legal systems of the world into the following eight families: Romanistic, Germanic, Nordic, common law, plus the law of the People's Republic of China, Japanese law, Islamic law and Hindu law.

Taking some of the existing classifications into account, we propose a division of the legal systems of the world into five large groups:

1.   Civil law, which includes the Romanistic and Germanic legal systems,
2.   Common law,
3.   Legal systems of the Muslim countries, or Islamic family,
4.   Eastern European legal systems: Russia and other legal systems highly influenced by the Russian system, and
5.   Asian legal systems.

Although this classification is not exhaustive, it is highly convenient from a linguistic point of view in that it covers most of the major legal translation combinations of the world. In addition, there are also some 'hybrid' legal systems that share characteristics from various legal systems. This is the case, for instance, of Scotland, the French province of Québec in Canada, Puerto Rico, the State of Louisiana in the United States or the Philippines, amongst others.

It is important for translators to be able to identify the main features of the legal families and systems to which their texts belong, as this will allow them to approach the texts with greater ease. Once translators have developed the appropriate strategies and techniques to approach a legal text and its difficulties, no matter with which legal system they are working, they can apply these strategies to their new legal system, provided they master the language and have at least a basic knowledge of that new culture.

This volume deals with the Western legal traditions, that is, the civil law and the common law. A brief overview of both families will be given below whilst Parts II and III of the book (Chapters 3 to 9) will cover several legal systems belonging to these two traditions. A broad range of language and culture combinations is thus covered and, as stated before, the strategies and techniques developed by translators having any of the cultures covered in the book as either source or target cultures can also be applied to any other linguistic or cultural combination.

2.2 The civil law tradition

In this section we describe the history and the main characteristics of the civil law family or tradition. The civil law system is considered to be the oldest legal family of the world and groups those countries where law has been formed on the basis of Roman law. More than a thousand years of evolution have notably changed both procedural and substantive law since that time.[1] The civil law family today is widely spread all over the world, from Europe to Japan or Indonesia. However, law in these countries does not share as many similarities as we may think and it is possible to find several sub-groupings within the family, e.g. Germanic law, Scandinavian law or the law of Latin American countries. This enormous expansion of the civil law family is mainly due to two factors: colonization by the Europeans and codification, a legal technique used by Romanistic laws during the nineteenth century that contributed to the expansion of Roman law.

What we know today as civil law originated in the twelfth century, after a period of accumulation of the various elements that were to form it. The renaissance of the study of Roman law in universities marked the start of a second period during the fourteenth and fifteenth centuries, which lasted for five centuries and which was characterized by the development of written law by jurists, under the influence of whom legal doctrine developed to reach the third and last period, where we are now and which started around the nineteenth century, defined by a clear predominance of legislation (David and Brierley 1985: 35).

One common characteristic shared by the legal systems belonging to the civil law tradition and, particularly, to the Romanistic family, is that law is understood as a set of fundamental principles and the approach to law is quite abstract, contrary to what happens in the common law tradition.

---

1 Procedural law, also termed adjective or remedial law, 'is that which prescribes methods of enforcing rights or obtaining redress for their invasion' (Black 1991: 1203) and is formed by the set of rules that govern the proceedings of the court. Substantive law is 'that part of law which creates, defines, and regulates rights and duties of parties' (*ibid.*: 1429).

In countries where the civil law family is applied, law concerns the whole of society and is not seen as a discipline isolated from other intellectual disciplines, but as the study of political, social and economic sciences and public administration, and focusing on the rights and duties recognized in society according to an ideal of justice. As Dadomo and Farran (1996) point out, because each individual is recognized as having rights, the law has an important educative role to play in society. Emphasis is therefore placed on the importance of the rule of law, the safeguarding of individual rights and accessibility to the law by lay people.

Another feature of these legal systems is the concept of legal rule, different to that existing in common law countries. In the Romanistic family, the law is formulated by the legislators and it seeks to cover general principles, not specific cases, working at an abstract and general level. Judges are then called to apply the law to the specific facts brought before them but they do not create law, they implement it.

As for the classification and structure of law in these countries, the Roman distinction between legal institutions which dealt with matters of public interest and those which were of private interest is also found at the origin of the current differentiation between public and private law. Public law refers to the relationship between the Government and the governed, whilst private law relates to matters arising between private individuals, whether they be citizens or corporate bodies/legal entities. The major areas of public law are constitutional law, administrative law, financial law and criminal law, although the latter overlaps in some aspects with private law as it protects individuals' rights, lives, property and so on. As for private law, it mainly covers civil law, understood as the regulation of the private relationships between individuals imposing reciprocal obligations and rights; commercial or business law, and labour law.

The sources of law tend to be organized in a similar manner in all the countries belonging to the civil law family. Legislation, in the strict sense, together with other rules or norms emanating from the legislative or even the executive powers, are the primary, almost exclusive, source of law. All countries belonging to this family have constitutions, codes and enacted legislation. Due to political and philosophical reasons, in these countries there is a common assumption that the best way to administer justice, the main *raison-d'être* of a legal system, is to apply (and assure the enforcement of) enacted law.

Customary law, understood as the law or general rule that arises from repeating a particular practice in like circumstances, has a secondary role to that of legislation in these countries, though on some occasions it is necessary to take a look at customary rules to clarify the ideas of legislators and thus be able to understand the legislation.

The role of case law[2] in these countries can be understood only when put into perspective regarding legislation. Judges can only interpret legislation but they cannot create law and that is why case law cannot be considered as a source of law in these countries. Similarly, legal doctrine, understood as scholarly writings, is not a source of law in these countries either, though some authors such as David and Brierley (1985: 147) consider it as a living and relevant source of law, stating that legal doctrine:

> is now, as in the past, a very important, living, source of law. This is shown by the fact that it creates the legal vocabulary and ideas which legislators subsequently use; it is even more evident from the fact that doctrinal writing establishes the methods by which law will be understood and statutes interpreted.

The last source of law in this family is general principles of law; basic rules and principles of justice with a general or abstract content applied universally in all legal systems of the world and usually expressed as a maxim or simple concept. The importance of these principles in the civil law tradition relies on the fact that there is a subordination of law to justice, and that law in these countries is not just a set of legal rules.

2   'The aggregate of reported cases as forming a body of jurisprudence, or the law of a particular subject as evidenced or formed by the adjudged cases, in distinction to statutes and other sources of law' (Black 1991: 216).

2.3 The common law tradition

Before entering into a discussion on the history and main characteristics of the common law family, it is useful to start by defining what is meant by the term 'common law' in these pages. Quoting De Cruz (2007: 102), it may refer to different realities:

1. the English legal system developed in, applicable to and common to England (and Wales, but not Scotland);
2. that part of English law which was created by the King's courts, or common law courts (and developed as case law) in England from about the twelfth century, rather than 'statute law', or the law enacted by Parliament as opposed to the body of rules and principles of equity, as established by decisions of the courts of equity (or, as they were otherwise known, Courts of Chancery), which began to be developed from around the fourteenth century;
3. the modern usage, which includes English cases and statutes, including principles developed and established by common law courts and the courts of equity; and
4. that part of English law which has been 'received' by a given jurisdiction and which applies therein, either through colonization or via unilateral and voluntary enactment by that jurisdiction.

'Common law' is thus a broad term that can be used to denote different concepts, all of them derived from the same reality, i.e. a legal system originated in England and exported to other parts of the world. As far as history is concerned, the common law system is considered to have existed since time immemorial and it is possible to trace back the origin of a common law in England to the twelfth century. Today, the common law family extends throughout the world, due mainly to British colonization and the dominance of the British Empire during key periods in history. Thus, this system of law can be nowadays found in countries such as the United States, Australia, India, Pakistan, Hong Kong, large parts of Africa, New Zealand,

Singapore, Canada (although the Canadian French region of Québec has a legal system based on the civil law tradition) or Malaysia, for example.

To understand the origin of the common law system it is necessary to recall some key moments in English history. In 1066 the Normans, under William I, defeated the Anglo-Saxons at the Battle of Hastings, leading to the subsequent gradual domination of the British Isles by the Normans. Previous legal practices had existed in England, some even written, but the effect of the Norman Conquest was so important that these practices disappeared. William I established a feudal system, with the King as the supreme lord, in which he took exclusive jurisdiction over all serious crimes and during the twelfth and thirteenth centuries a general jurisdiction was implemented. Three permanent central courts, i.e. the royal courts, were established in Westminster, leading to the centralization of justice in England and the unification of English law.

Litigation in the middle ages was based on writs, 'a command of the King directed to the relevant official, judge or magistrate, containing a brief indication of a matter under dispute and instructing the addressee to call the defendant into his court and to resolve the dispute in the presence of the parties' (Zweigert and Kötz 1998: 184). Towards the end of the fourteenth century the methods of the royal courts were criticized as the application of the law was considered to be too rigid. Technical errors or problems of procedure caused the parties who had lost their suit to address the King asking him to ignore the rules of the common law and to apply moral and good conscience. The King transmitted these petitions to the Chancellor, who knew the common law well as he was the 'keeper of the King's conscience', and he issued the writs (*ibid.*: 187). The Chancellor then decided the case in equity, in fairness, so developing a parallel system of law based on a practical approach.[3] Until the nineteenth century, equity could only be administered by the Courts of Chancery, in London; equity and common law were applied in different courts and

---

3   Equity was understood at this time as a set of maxims of fairness. The concept has evolved and it is now understood as 'a part of substantive law distinguished from the rest by the fact that it was developed by the decisions of a particular court, the Court of Chancery' (*ibid.:* 188).

they were not contradictory, rather complementary to those of common law. The Supreme Court of Judicature Acts of 1873–1875 fused the rules of common law and equity in their jurisdictional application, though they still exist as separate bodies of law which can now be used and applied by the same courts (De Cruz 2007: 101).

Today, the British Isles host different legal systems due to the historical evolution of the various territories. Scotland, an independent kingdom from England until the eighteenth century, developed a legal system under Roman influence, due to its alliance with France and Holland, which is still maintained today and which blends common law and Roman law.

The Channel Islands of Jersey and Guernsey also have their own legal system based on Norman customary law, as is also the case in Northern Ireland, where a common law system has operated since the partition of Ireland in 1921. As a result, the Republic of Ireland also developed its own legal system which is analysed in Chapter 9.

According to De Cruz (2007: 103–4), the common law tradition has a series of characteristics, which can be defined as follows:

1. a case-based system of law, which functions through analogical reasoning;
2. a hierarchical doctrine of precedent;
3. sources of law that include statutes as well as cases;
4. typical institutions such as the trust, tort law, estoppel, and agency [...];
5. a distinctive improvisatory and pragmatic legal style;
6. categories of law, such as contract and tort, as separate bodies of law as well as two main bodies of law, common law and equity, which may, nevertheless, be administered by the same court.

One of the main features of the common law tradition is the case-based system, where decisions of higher courts are binding on lower courts and so create the doctrine of precedent, according to which a court should apply the rulings of previous cases in situations with similar facts. However, case law is not the only source of law today and statute law, or legislation (law enacted by a legislature or other governing body), now plays a dominant role, although the English legal attitude towards statutes is often that they are passed to clarify or consolidate existing law and to build on existing case law.

Another characteristic of common law is its pragmatic and, to a certain extent, improvisatory style aimed at the expeditious resolution of disputes as a means to providing remedies for specific cases. Furthermore, when adjudicating disputes judges formulate rules of law that they apply to specific and concrete situations. This is due to the fact that English law is not codified in the civil sense of being contained in enacted collections of exhaustive rules of law (*ibid.*) and therefore law is not as rigid as it may be considered to be in civil law countries. Hence, whilst in civil law countries lawyers and judges think more in terms of solving problems derived from systematic approaches to the law and they work towards general solutions and principles, English judges pay special attention to individual cases and facts.

Finally, the law is not organized on a public/private basis, as occurs in civil law countries, even if this distinction is recognized in countries belonging to the common law tradition. Contrary to what happens in countries following the Continental (civil law) tradition, separate courts for private and public law cases do not exist in common law. It is however more usual to differentiate between civil law and criminal law on the grounds of whether the purpose is to facilitate the interaction between individuals (civil law) or to enforce particular standards of behaviour (criminal law).

PART II

The Civil Law Tradition

In this part, several legal systems belonging to the civil law tradition are analysed in a succinct way so that the information may be used in translator training. During the initial stages of education, trainee translators do not normally have a thorough knowledge of the legal systems to which the texts they translate belong to, but they must at least be able to grasp the main features of these legal systems and have the necessary competence to do research and find the information needed to correctly understand source texts and produce accurate and high quality target texts. In later stages of training they will be able to go into further detail according to their needs. For this reason, we have identified some main aspects that translators should be aware of about the legal systems with which they work: the historical evolution of the legal system, the organization of law, sources of law, system of courts, and the legal profession. We have decided not to include aspects related to any particular branch of law, such as family law, contract law or criminal law, as the enormous range of texts translators are faced with in their daily practice make it impossible to decide which branch or which text type could be most usefully described. However, we agree with Mattila (2006: 266) that there is 'a need for systematic study and comparison of legal institutions and concepts and their designations, from the standpoint of many languages, in defined domains' and we believe that research on the topic must be encouraged. To partially cover this dearth of comparative analyses at a micro-level, we have included some examples and exercises in Chapter 11, where different branches of law and text types are introduced.

As outlined in the Introduction, Chapter 3 is dedicated to the Italian legal system, a direct heir of Roman law; Chapter 4 focuses on France, as it can be considered the parent legal system of some of the legal systems of the Romanistic family and is present in some of the legal systems of the Islamic family; Chapter 5 deals with Spain as it strongly influences other legal systems in Latin America, and Chapter 6 discusses Germany, the parent legal system of the Germanistic family. In line with David and Brierley (1985), we consider that the legal systems belonging to the Romanistic and to the Germanistic families have more rather than less in common, this being the reason for including them together under the same legal tradition.

CHAPTER 3

Italy

By Angela Carpi

Historically, Italian law is grounded in classical Roman law, as happens with the other systems belonging to the civil law tradition and as opposed to the common law tradition. As we will see below, the modern shape of Italian law is the result of several different influences (Sacco 1991), mainly French codification and German legal reasoning. But the result, nowadays, is an autonomous system with its own peculiarities and developments.

The elements analysed in this chapter are as follows: the formation of the Italian legal system and its evolution, its organization in the country, the different sources of law, the court system and, finally, the legal professions in Italy.

3.1 Historical evolution of the Italian legal system

Italian law, like most civil law traditions, can be said to have various origins but, in particular, to have descended from classical Roman law, which became with time *jus civile* and can be distinguished in many ways from the common law. The Italian legal tradition draws its sources from ancient Roman law (i.e. *Institutiones*, *Digesta*, *Codex* and *Novellae*) and substantially still mirrors those ancient principles today, albeit filtered through the experience of the Medieval and Renaissance jurists, and later summarized in the French Napoleon codification of 1804, which in Italy was partially affected by the influx of German doctrine based on the study of Pandects.[1]

Modern Italian law finds its origins in medieval Roman law that experienced the rebirth of ancient Roman law through its study in Northern Italy, starting in Bologna, during the twelfth century, thanks to the work of Irnerio and the school of Glossators (Lambertini 2006; Bellodi Ansaloni 2015). The latter were scholars who applied the method of interlinear or marginal annotation, known as *glossae*, in the interpretation of the Justinian code. Initially, this was a simple style exercise, since that law was not applied, only studied. This is at the origin of the theoretical study at universities that, starting with Irnerio and his school, extended all over Europe (Dalla 2004).

In the middle of the thirteenth century, Franciscus Accursius, a professor at Bologna and the last of the glossators, undertook the task of collecting and organizing the vast number of annotations made by his predecessors in one complete work. This compilation, the *glossa ordinaria*, supplemented by the annotations of Accursius himself, was known as the *glossa magna*. The glossators laid the foundations for the study of Roman law in Europe at a time when increasing commercial relations between individuals and states were soon to require an advanced legal system.

Their discussions tended to be academic rather than practical and it was the task of their successors of the fourteenth century, the commentators or postglossators, to effect a closer liaison between the revived Roman law and the law of the Italian cities, and to find a way to apply Roman law to the practical legal needs of the day.

On the eve of the modern period in Italy's history, which was to start in the nineteenth century, its legal system had become a *mélange* of

---

1   The German Pandectist School (so called because it was based on the most important body of the Roman legal sources: the Digest, from the Greek *Pandectae*), aimed at a dogmatic and systematic study of Roman legal material. Its learning was deep, exact, and abstract. The application of law was a technical process and legal thinking was based on prioritizing conceptual calculus over careful observation of social reality. The Pandectist School produced a method of studying law which was common to the whole of Germany in the nineteenth century.

sophisticated and advanced Roman/Canon law evolved from medieval scholarship and combined, where apt or necessary, with customary law and communal statutory compilations (Grossi 2006). The fragmented social and economic structure of the entire peninsula, combined with a certain political and governmental disunity, had produced an additional mass of unfocused and disparate legislation that was constantly in the process of promulgation and development by a number of bodies. However even though the values of the Enlightenment era influenced the evolution of societal and economic development in the Italian system, the condition existing in 1800 could not be called 'modern', as the evolution of the Italian legal system was not yet completed. We had to wait for at least another century for that (Grossi 2012).

Modern and contemporary Italian law cannot be said to be an original product, since it has been strongly influenced first by the French civil code and, to a lesser extent, by German codification and legal theory. The influence of the French Revolution spread both because of the prestige of the ideas of 1789 and because of Napoleon's political expansion and conquest. We may say that in all the autonomous states that formed Italy in 1815, a civil code based on the French *code civil* was in force. After unity, in 1861, a civil code was drafted and approved in 1865 and the influence of the French model is evident in this first codification.

A second important stage can be established around 1920, when the Italian legal scholarship had come under the spell of the German Pandectists. Italian law has always been responsive to doctrine and the writings of university professors and these Germanic influences had the effect of drawing the Italian system away from the analytical approach of the French scholars and towards the conceptualism and dogmatism of the German school. The legislation of the fascist period, beginning with the criminal code of 1930 and concluding with the new civil code of 1942 – still in force – was influenced by fascist ideology but only to a certain degree. The latter, together with the civil procedure code, also of 1942, were the product of relatively disinterested scholars and contain little that can be attributed to any fascist concepts. While political conditions may have influenced the development of public law and introduced changes into the criminal codes, there is little evidence of any fascist pressures or theory in the vast recodification of private law (Padoa Schioppa 2007).

The 1942 civil code was (for its day) revolutionary, in that it combined, in a single compilation of 2,000 articles, the regulation of all aspects of private life, both civil and commercial, abrogating the 1865 civil code and the commercial code of 1882. The structure of the code was the most innovative facet, introducing a codification of private (non-governmental) aspects of labour law as well as an extensive codification of the rights of citizens and their protection. Unlike the nineteenth century version, it is strictly technical in its approach, eschewing doctrine and casuistry. Although a product of the fascist era, the Italian civil code has survived, though not without modification, and it served as the model for the new Dutch civil code as well as for several new Latin American legislative reforms.

The most recent change in Italian law came with the introduction of a new code of criminal procedure in 1988. This fact not only swept away the fascist-influenced criminal procedure code of 1930, but it also changed the entire approach of Italian criminal procedural law. Hitherto, Italian criminal procedure had been modelled on the French *code d'instruction criminelle* based on an inquisitorial system followed in most countries in Europe, both western and eastern. The new code, in a revolutionary about-turn, adopted the adversarial approach found in the Anglo-American system.

3.2 Organization of law

A first traditional distinction in the organization of Italian law is between public and private law. The terminology derives directly from Roman law, but its meaning has changed over time. In general terms, it can be said that private law is the law that regulates the relations between individuals, whilst public law regulates relations where, in some ways, the state is part. Public law regulates the organization of the state and other public authorities; it establishes the rules of the organization of public entities and of the behaviour of citizens. There are several areas of public law, such as constitutional law, administrative law, criminal law, and financial and tax law, whereas private law concerns civil matters such as family law, commercial and business law, labour law, competition law and corporate law, among others.

The above-mentioned distinction is however highly variable and not at all static. It deals with theoretical categories of the law and is therefore a typical product of all the systems belonging to the civil law tradition. The state could, indeed, maintain the performance of functions that were once attributed to private subjects or vice versa, it could give some activity up in favour of private bodies. So, not everything that concerns public bodies belongs to public law (i.e. the university rental of a building through a contract of private law) and it may be that the same event is regulated by both public and private law rules: a car that runs over a pedestrian gives rise to both a criminal law and a private action (*azione per lesioni personali colpose* and *azione per il risarcimento del danno*).

In conclusion, it can be said that the traditional distinction *publicum ius est quod ad statum rei romanae spectat, privatum quod ad singulorum utilitatem*[2] is quite evanescent and it can be maintained as a general principle, but for the analysis of legal reality, it is necessary to determine the value and importance of the various interests involved.

3.3 Sources of law in Italy

The mass of Italian legislation is quite intimidating; the body of national and regional laws and regulations and their accompanying judicial exegesis may seem overwhelming. Ordinary legislation originates in the national parliament, which is a bicameral legislature with a long history of extensive

---

2   Public law concerns the Roman State, private law concerns individuals.

publications. The 20 regions that form the Italian state also have varying degrees of legislative power and take advantage of it, restricted only in that their laws may not conflict with 'fundamental national interest'. Five of the regions (Valle d'Aosta, Trentino – Alto Adige, Friuli – Venezia Giulia, Sardegna and Sicilia) enjoy a greater degree of autonomy than the rest.

The hierarchy of the sources of Italian law is firstly established in the civil code of 1942. Art. 1 of the so called *preleggi*, a book of the civil code that contains indications on the law in general, organizes the sources of the law indicating, in the first place, the *leggi*, followed by *regolamenti* of the government, then the *norme corporative*, nowadays called *contratti collettivi* and, finally, customs. With the end of the fascist era, guild contracts lost part of their importance, whilst the other sources of law maintained their influence and order in the hierarchy. In 1948, though, a new important source entered into force: the Constitution, where the hierarchy of internal sources of law was partially revised. Firstly, we can now find principles that are defined as supreme or fundamental, from which inviolable rights derive (art. 2 of the Italian Constitution), therefore the norms that contains such principles are unalterable. Secondly, there are the *leggi costituzionali*. Thirdly, we find the statutes enacted by the parliament, *leggi statali ordinarie* and the other sources of art. 1 of the *preleggi*. In case of conflict of laws, two main rules apply: the law that is hierarchically higher prevails; among rules that belong to the same level, the most recent one approved prevails.

As is clear from the above-mentioned description, the hierarchy of Italian law is not without its own complexity. At the apex, we find the *Constituzione* of 1948. It is a fairly rigid document, not subject to casual amendment. The *leggi costituzionali*, which are amendatory, must, in effect, be passed twice by both houses (*Parlamento* and *Senato)*, first by simple majority and second by absolute majority. Next are *leggi*, ordinary laws passed by the president. After the latter, there are the *decreti legislativi*, acts decreed by ministers of the government in accordance with powers delegated by the parliament in a specific piece of legislation. Along with these we find the *decreti legge*, decrees issued by the government that must be approved by the parliament within sixty days of their issuance or they lose their validity. They then either become *legge* or remain, when signed by the president, *decreti del Presidente della Repubblica*. The hierarchy referred

to above is not absolute. Laws and acts having the force of law differ in that they result from different procedures; however they substantially have the same authority.

This hierarchy deals with internal sources of the law, but, since Italy is a Member of the European Union, EU law is also a source of law in Italy. EU law sources can be distinguished in directives and regulations. The latter are directly applicable in the member states and are binding in their entirety (art. 249 § 2 of the Treaty establishing the EC). Directives, on the other hand, 'shall be binding, as to the result to be achieved, upon each MS to which it is addressed, but shall leave to the national authorities the choice of forms and methods' (art. 249 § 1 of the same Treaty).

The Italian *Corte Costituzionale* (see Section 3.4) has clarified that, in cases of conflict of rules between a European regulation and an Italian internal law, the Italian judge should apply the European rule, even if the Italian internal rule is more recent, placing the European legislation in a hierarchically higher position than the internal law. In a hierarchically lower position than ordinary law, we find customary law. The latter can have effects only if it is not contrary to ordinary law, nevertheless, it has some importance both historically, in the formation of the Italian legal system, and in some areas of contemporary private law, especially for those matters that do not have any regulation under ordinary law.

Another source of law in Italy is international law set by international treaties. There are two different kinds of international treaties in which Italy is a party. The first category are treaties that need to be ratified, approved and published by the Italian Government in order to be enforceable in Italy. In this case, the law that ratifies the international treaty is ordinary internal law and it is treated as any other ordinary law. The second kind of international treaty is the self-executing treaty, directly applied in the state that signed the treaty, for instance, The Vienna Convention on International Sale of Goods of 1980, signed by Italy in 1988. This kind of treaty is considered internal law, enforceable without the need for further ratification by the national government.

Finally it is necessary to mention case law. Italy being a civil law country does not recognize any binding authority to precedent, even if emanating from higher courts. However, decisions coming from the *Corte di Cassazione* are persuasive for lower courts and can influence their decisions.

3.4 The Italian court system

The Italian legal system has adopted a unique method for allocating jurisdiction, centred on the nature of the subjective legal situation: if an individual right is violated, the *giustizia ordinaria* will be in charge. If a collective interest is violated, the case will be allocated to the *giustizia amministrativa*.

3.4.1 Ordinary jurisdiction

The judicial power in Italy is exercised by different judges and courts. Both civil and criminal cases fall under the umbrella of the *giustizia ordinaria*. The civil jurisdiction is made up of the *giudici di pace*; the *tribunali* at first instance, and for revision of decisions of *giudici di pace* at second instance and the *corti d'appello* for revision of decisions of *tribunali* (see Table 1). At the base of the court system are the *giudici di pace*, who can decide on claims up to 5,000 euros, though the limit can rise up to 20,000 euros when the matter deals with the circulation of vehicles and has no limits in some specific matters indicated by the law (art. 7 Italian code of civil procedure). They are lay judges, located in each of Italy's more than 8,000 communes. The superior courts of first instance are the *tribunali*, which serve as appellate courts from the lower judiciary and also, with the participation of lay judges, as criminal courts. The *corti d'appello* are assigned one to each region, although some larger regions have two or more, and they have direct jurisdiction in matters concerning the recognition and enforcement of foreign judgements. At the apex is the *Corte di Cassazione*, which is the final appellate court in all civil and criminal cases.

Table 1: Italian civil courts

Corti d'Appello	Second instance for revision of decisions of the *tribunal*.
Tribunali	Second instance for revision of decisions of the *giudici di pace*. First instance in other cases.
Giudici di pace	First instance for claims up to €5,000 (€20,000 if matter on circulations of vehicles).

The courts found for criminal Jurisdiction at first instance are the *procura*, the *tribunale* and the *corte d'assise* for special matters. At second Instance there are the *corte d'assise d'appello* and the *corti d'appello*. These are courts that deal with specific criminal cases, indicated in art. 5 of the Italian code of criminal procedure. The composition of the *corte d'assise* is mixed: there are eight members, two ordinary judges and six jurors, chosen among citizens aged between thirty and sixty-five years old. Both ordinary judges and jurors are part of the body that will decide the case before them.

The *giustizia ordinaria* is administered by 'professional' and 'honorary' judges, who form part of the judiciary (art. 4 of Royal Decree no. 12 of January 1941). Honorary judges are:

1. *Giudice di pace*: competent, both in civil and criminal law, for matters previously dealt with by professional judges.
2. *Giudici onorari*: personnel who did not complete the career for appointment as a judge. They are attached to the temporary divisions named *Sezioni stralcio* and can deal with the civil cases pending on 30 April 1995.
3. *Giudici onorari di tribunal*: attached to the judicial offices.
4. *Procuratori onorari aggiunti*: attached to the prosecuting offices.
5. *Esperti* of the courts and the juvenile divisions of the courts of appeal.
6. *Giurati* of the *corti d'assise*.
7. *Esperti* working for the *tribunale di sorveglianza*.

3.4.2 Administrative jurisdiction

The term *giustizia amministrativa* refers to the instruments of the legal system for the protection of private subjects against the public administration. There is a separate structure of administrative courts, which are branches of the executive department rather than part of the judiciary system. Each region has a regional administrative court named *tribunale amministrativo regionale* (*TAR*) with competence to hear a wide range of administrative questions. The final court of appeal for administrative matters is the *Consiglio di Stato*; appeals from this court can be filed to a special section of the *Corte di Cassazione*, but are rare and would only involve questions of jurisdiction.

3.4.3 *Other courts*

The *Corte Costituzionale* is a separate body, independent of the professional judiciary, and deals with judicial review of legislation. This court is also in charge of decisions concerning conflicts of attribution between the state and the regions and sits as a criminal court for crimes charged against a Ministry of the Italian Republic in the execution of its functions and against the President of the Italian Republic. Only judges can refer a case to the Constitutional Court.

In addition, there is tax jurisdiction, where first and second instance courts can be found: the *commissioni tributarie provinciali* and the *commissioni tributarie regionali*, respectively.

The audit jurisdiction consists of a *Corte dei conti*, with the function of administrative control and supervision over taxes, revenue and expenditures within the budget of the state. It sits at single sessions at first instance and at plenary sessions at second instance, and it deals with the control of the accounts of the state and of the regional bodies.

The military jurisdiction has a specific remit in times of war, established by the law, and in times of peace it deals only with crimes committed by military personnel. This jurisdiction consists of a *Tribunale Militare* at first instance and a *Corte Militare d'Appello* at second instance. Finally, there is also a juvenile jurisdiction. The table below shows the structure and levels of the various courts in Italy (see Table 2).

Table 2: Italian court system

	GIUSTIZIA AMMINISTRATIVA	*GIUSTIZIA ORDINARIA*	
SECONDO GRADO	*Consiglio di Stato*	*Corte di Cassazione*	
	TAR Lazio	*Corti d'appello* *Corti d'assise d'appello*	
PRIMO GRADO	*Tribunali amministrativi regionali (TAR)*	*PENALE*	*CIVILE*
		Corti d'assise	*Tribunale*
		Tribunale	
		Tribunale di sorveglianza	
		Procura	*Tribunale del lavoro*
		Giudice di pace	

3.5 The legal professions in Italy

A number of different legal professions exist in Italy and a distinction can be made between those linked to the judiciary and other professions.

3.5.1 The judiciary

The jurisdiction analysed above in Section 3.4 is operated in Italy by *mag-istrati* or *giudici*, who are appointed after having passed a national, very selective examination. The independence of the judges is one of the main principles on which the Italian democratic state is based. The judiciary is autonomous *vis-à-vis* the executive and its independence would be under-mined if measures pertaining to the career advancement of its members, and in more general terms, their *status*, were assigned to the executive power. The Constitution therefore assigns the task of administering the members of the judiciary to the self-governing body (art. 105 Const.) of *Consiglio Superiore della Magistratura*, which oversees appointments, transfers, promotions, assignments of duties and disciplinary actions.

The judiciary is also autonomous vis-à-vis the legislative power, in that judges are subject only to the law (art. 101 of the Italian Constitution). The Constitution (art. 104) establishes that the *Consiglio Superiore della Magistratura* is made up of three members by right:

1. the President of the Republic, who presides over the body,
2. the President of the *Corte Suprema di Cassazione*, and
3. the *Procuratore generale* of the *Corte Suprema di Cassazione*.

The Constitution does not establish the number of elected members but it does state that two thirds of them must be elected by all ordinary judges belonging to the various categories, the so-called *membri togati*, and one third by parliament in a joint session. The candidates must be chosen from among all the ordinary university law professors and lawyers who have at least fifteen years of experience in their profession, the so called *membri laici*. The Constitution also states that the elected members will hold their seats for four years and that they cannot be re-elected immediately. It is therefore the *legge ordinaria* that determines both the number of elected members and the way in which they are designated.

Currently, *Legge* 44/2002 establishes the number of elected members at 24, 16 of whom are stipendiary and 8 lay; the latter are elected by parliament in a joint session by secret ballot and with a three fifths majority of the assembly members for the first two ballots, whilst the third ballot only requires three fifths of the votes.

There is a further distinction between the *magistratura giudicante*, who administer justice, and the *magistratura inquirente*, who prosecute and defend public interests, both in criminal and civil law. The judges, who form the *magistratura giudicante*, are called to judge and to file a decision, in civil or criminal matters, at the end of the procedure and after having heard parties and lawyers, whereas the *pubblico ministero* or *magistratura inquirente* is responsible for representing the interests of the state and of society in civil law matters and in criminal proceedings.

As in the French legal system, which is described in Chapter 4, the office of the public prosecutor in Italy is organized in *procuratori, avvocati dello Stato* and *sostituti procuratori della Repubblica*, depending on their rank and on the court where they perform their functions.

In the administration and organization of courts, another important profession is that of the *cancelliere*, an official in charge of the practical organization of the courts. The Italian name, *cancellieri*, and the function of these officials derive from canon law that historically strongly influenced the development of law in Italy. The translation of the term *cancelliere* for 'clerk of court' might be misleading, since the latter in the common law system has more responsibilities than the Italian *cancelliere*. In addition to running the court, the *cancelliere* is in charge of the organization and transcription of the hearing and of the publication of the decision of the judge, but is not necessarily a professional with a degree in Law.

The *polizia giudiziaria*, the criminal investigation department of the police, are also part of the court officials, and are in charge of conducting the investigation in criminal law cases and they work together with the appointed judge.

3.5.2 *Other legal professions*

The most popular legal profession in Italy is probably that of *avvocato*, one of the most ancient intellectual professions, and is based on the clients' need to receive advice during a proceeding in order to protect their own rights. No particular specialization is needed to give extra-judiciary advice, though to represent a client before a judge it is necessary to be an *avvocato*. Lawyers begin their career with a degree in Law and then have to work as *praticante* in the office of an appointed lawyer for at least eighteen months. After this period, it is possible to sit for the *esame di abilitazione alla professione forense*, the passing of which allows them to be registered in the formal *albo degli avvocati*, held by the local branch of the Italian bar association. Enrolment in the register of lawyers is compulsory to be able to practise the profession, as well as enrolment in the *Cassa Forense*, the special social security service for lawyers.

The *codice deontologico* regulates their activity and states the rules of conducts of the *avvocato*. The *avvocato* can plead in any court except the *Corte di Cassazione* and the *Consiglio di Stato*, where it is necessary to be a *cassazionista*.[3] To be able to plead before the higher jurisdictions, it is necessary to sit a specific examination. A lawyer is restricted to work in the territory covered by the *albo degli avvocati* and pleading in a court outside the mentioned territory can only be done with the support of a *domiciliatario* or local colleague.

Another important legal profession, typical of the civil law tradition, is that of the *notaio*, who in Italy is a public officer that holds the seal of the notaries. In order to be appointed as a *notaio* it is necessary to sit a specific examination. In the Roman culture, the notaries were the clerks who acted as scribes for the emperor. Nowadays, notaries draft and are compelled to keep deeds, wills and all sort of public acts in their legal custody. As a public officer, notaries perform public functions as they are vested by the state with public authority, which allows them to draw up authentic, therefore reliable deeds and acts.

3   The *cassazionista* is a lawyer that has the possibility to defend clients in higher jurisdictions (*Corte Suprema di Cassazione, Consiglio di Stato*). Until 2014, there were two possibilities for a lawyer to become a *cassazionista*: to sit a specific examination or to have spent twelve years enrolled in the *albo degli avvocati*. Since 2015 a new *legge professionale* has been in force, making it compulsory to take a specific exam in order to become a *cassazionista*.

CHAPTER 4

France

This chapter offers an overview of the historical evolution of the French legal system along with an explanation of its organization, an account of its sources of law as well as a description of the French court system and the legal professions in this country.

4.1 Historical evolution of the French legal system

As happens with all legal systems belonging to the Romanistic Family, French law originates from Roman law, which strongly influenced its structure and form. After the collapse of the Roman Empire in the fifth century, some Roman sources were summarized and commented, which contributed to the survival of some knowledge of Roman law in the southern part of France. In the north, however, the incursion of the Franks brought with them their own customary laws of Germanic origin. Some centuries later, in the eleventh and twelfth centuries, the renaissance of Roman law studies in the north of Italy was followed by an interest in the study of Law in the south of France, particularly at the universities of Montpellier and Toulouse. It was precisely in France where the School of the Commentators was born. These jurists 'sought to apply and adapt Roman law [...] to the needs and conditions of medieval life, particularly with a view to establishing a unified system of law from the mixture of customary law, canon law, municipal law and the law of the Empire' (Dadomo and Farran 1996: 4). In practice, the French territory was divided into two areas for legal purposes: the area of *droit écrit* in the south, influenced by Roman law, and the area of *droit coutumier* in the north, influenced by German customs, although both territories shared part of the law of the other and customary law gradually became written law.

During the sixteenth century, and due mainly to Roman law and its *Corpus Iuris Civilis* along with barbarian codes and the codes of customary law, there was strong support for the development of a common private law contained in a code. The *Coutume de Paris*, a compilation of customary law published in 1510 under the French parliament and reissued in 1580, together with commentaries stressing the idea of generally applicable and universal principles of law for the whole of France during the sixteenth, seventeenth and eighteenth centuries, also led to the development of codes. Codification was also encouraged by legal philosophers of the natural law school, who believed in 'independent and autonomous principles of nature from which could be inferred a system of legal rules' (*ibid.*: 8).

After the French Revolution in 1789 and during the ten years before Napoleon's rise to power in 1799, France went through the period of the *Droit Intermédiaire*. All the institutions of the *Ancien Régime* were abolished (absolute powers of monarchy, the nobility, the clergy, the judiciary, the feudal system, etc.) and equality was sought, with the aim of establishing a civil code common to all. When Napoleon took power in 1799 he took over the project and in 1804 the French civil code, named *Code civil des Français*, was promulgated. The code did not represent a total break with the past, but it introduced a new legal and judicial organization. Although more than two centuries have passed since the promulgation of the French civil code and several reforms have taken place, and are still taking place, the Napoleonic code is the key stone of French law today.

The codification process had an impact in Europe and some countries felt the legacy, not only of Roman law but also of French codification, leading to a distinction between codified and non-codified systems of law, thus differentiating between common law and civil law systems.

4.2 Organization of law

France, as all legal systems belonging to the civil law family, distinguishes between public and private law to differentiate the sphere of matters of public interest and those regulating the lives of individuals. Nonetheless, there is an internal division in French law between the *ordre judiciaire* and the *ordre administratif* based on the principle of separation of powers which appears in the French statute of 16–24 August 1790, according to which, ordinary judges shall not interfere in any way whatsoever with the activities of public authorities, nor hear a claim brought against a public authority in relation to the performance of their official duties (Steiner 2010: 249).

The *ordre judiciaire* covers both civil and criminal jurisdictions, therefore mixing public and private affairs, although different courts in charge of civil and criminal matters exist. The *ordre administratif* regulates conflicts between different branches of the French public bodies or between the state and the individuals (see Figure 1).

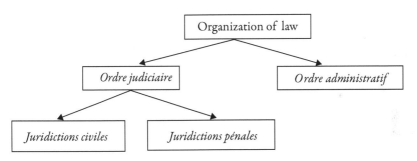

Figure 1: Organization of law in France.

4.3 Sources of law in France

Sources of law in France are divided between those which are authoritative and give rise to legal rules, the primary sources of law, and those which are persuasive and not binding, the subsidiary sources of law.

4.3.1 *Authoritative sources of law*

Authoritative sources of law include written laws and custom. The main source of law of the French legal system is written legislation, including international legislation (international treaties and conventions, European Union law) and domestic legislation. The latter includes the Constitution, the *règles à valeur legislative* (legislation enacted by the national parliament) the *règles à valeur réglamentaire* (legislation enacted by administrative authorities) and the *conventions collectives* (legislation that has a contractual origin; contracts signed by individuals, professional agreements or union contracts).

The existing set of written legislation is organized following a hierarchical order, and a newly enacted *loi* must always respect a series of principles, namely:

- it must respect former legislation of higher level;
- it can modify former legislation of the same level;
- it entails the derogation of former legislation of a lower level.

4.3.1.1 Written legislation

International sources of law

The international sources of law in France are the international treaties and agreements as well as European Union law. International treaties must be ratified or approved and published by the French government before coming into force. Some of the treaties are directly applied whilst others require that an internal norm or regulation be enacted so as to become enforceable.

As is the case in all member states of the European Union, EU law is a source of law in France and includes primary legislation (the treaties establishing the EU), secondary legislation (directives and regulations) and supplementary law (including case law, international law and general principles of EU law). Recommendations and decisions are nonbinding.

Domestic sources of law

The written sources of law in France are the *règles à valeur constitutionnelle*, the *règles à valeur legislative*, the *règles à valeur réglementaire* and the *conventions collectives*. The *règles à valeur constitutionnelle* are constitutional norms and include the current French Constitution of 4 October 1958, the Preamble to the Constitution of 27 October 1946, the Declaration of the Rights of Man and of the Citizen of 26 August 1789, the *Charte de l'environnement* of 2004, the fundamental principles recognized by the laws of the Republic and the principles and objectives with constitutional value. The *règles à valeur législative* include, in a hierarchical order, the *lois organiques* followed by the *lois ordinaires*. The domain of the latter is clearly established in the Constitution but there exists no specific list of subjects that must be regulated by a *loi organique*. The *lois ordinaires* are enacted following the normal legislative process and are the most numerous types of statutes in France. They cannot go against the *lois organiques* nor be unaware of them.

Of lesser importance than the constitutional norms and legislation is a third level of French sources of law, that of *règles à valeur réglamentaire*. These include *ordonnances*, legislation enacted by the executive branch thanks to an authorization of the parliament and *règlements*, whose object is to decide in areas not reserved to the legislative branch or to develop legal dispositions to ensure their application. Finally, the *conventions collectives* are agreements negotiated between the private sector social agents (employers and trade unions) to ensure respect for rights of employees in the private sector, under the general dispositions regulated in the labour code.

4.3.1.2 Custom

Custom, considered to be the second authoritative source of law in the
French legal system, originates from the people and it is safeguarded by
the state. David (1972: 170) defines custom as 'the continuing behaviour
over a period of time of those governed by the law, with the understanding
that their behaviour is required by the law'. Custom, which can be written or unwritten, must comply with certain requirements in order to be
recognized as a formal source of law:

> Firstly, it must evolve through a slow, but spontaneous process of development – it
> cannot consist of a single occurrence, or be imposed on people other than by their
> own will, but must evolve through imitation and repetition. Secondly, it must
> have popular support and consent as to its usage, i.e., social approval and consen-
> sus. Thirdly, the obligatory nature of a custom must be recognized in the way it
> is regarded. This is the intellectual or psychological factor, whereby a custom is
> invested with judicial conviction both by those subject to it and others (Dadomo
> and Farran, 1996: 39).

4.3.2 Subsidiary sources of law

The subsidiary sources of law in France are case law and doctrine, understood as the writings of legal scholars on legal matters. The decisions of
the courts do not have legal authority in the sense that they do not create
legislation. This is strictly stated in article 5 of the French civil code, which
prohibits the establishment of rules of precedent by judges. Judges do have
the obligation to rule upon all cases brought before them and to apply
legislation, in some cases interpreting what it says, but their decisions do
not become law. Therefore, former judicial decisions are not binding for
lower courts deciding on similar cases. Decisions from the Supreme Court
in civil and criminal matters, the *Cour de cassation*, can however influence
decisions of other courts.

The role of doctrine in French law is considered to be influential as far
as it consists of a systematic and critical exposition of positive law through
written commentary. It includes not only the work of scholars, but also that

of judges, practitioners and law teachers and it can be found in manuals, journals, doctoral theses and so on. Even if doctrine cannot be considered as a source of law strictly speaking, it is considered as an inspiration and influence to be referred to when there is no case law on a particular matter or when the existing case law is not satisfactory (Dadomo and Farran 1996: 44–5).

4.4 The French court system

As mentioned in Section 4.2, there is an internal division in French law between the civil and criminal branch, the *ordre judiciaire*, and the administrative branch, the *ordre administratif*, according to which, administrative courts cannot decide on civil and criminal cases and disputes involving the executive or administrative affairs cannot be heard by ordinary (civil and criminal) courts. As a result, there exists a dual system of courts in France which differentiates between administrative and ordinary matters. Therefore, the courts of the administrative branch are competent to decide on cases involving individuals and the state as such or any public authority (be it a public corporation, authority or civil servant). On the other hand, the ordinary courts adjudicate disputes between individuals in the area of civil law or punish offenders under criminal law. Within ordinary courts it is also possible to establish another difference between the general courts, *juridictions de droit commun*, and the specialized courts, *juridictions d'exception*. The table below shows the structure and levels of courts in France (see Table 3).

Table 3: French court system

	ORDRE ADMINISTRATIF	ORDRE JUDICIAIRE	
		TRIBUNAL DES CONFLITS	
HAUTES JURIDICTIONS	Conseil d'État	Cour de cassation	
DEUXIÉME DEGRÉ	Cour administrative d'appel	Cour d'appel / Cour d'assises (Pénal)	
PREMIER DEGRÉ		PÉNAL	CIVIL
			Tribunal de grande instance
	Autres juridictions administratives spécialisées	Cour d'assises	Tribunal d'instance
	Tribunaux administratifs	Tribunal correctionnel	Tribunal de commerce
		Tribunal de police	Conseil de prud'hommes
			Tribunal paritaire des baux ruraux
			Tribunal des affaires de sécurité sociale
		Juge de proximité	

The *tribunal des conflits* manages the existence of a dual system of courts reflecting the separation between administrative and ordinary courts. This court determines which branch is competent to decide when there is a conflict of jurisdiction between the courts of both branches. Likewise, it is for this court to solve the potential problem that may arise if two courts belonging to different branches take a decision on the same matter. This can happen when it is unclear whether an action should be brought before an administrative or an ordinary court and also when in some cases courts have a different interpretation as to the scope of their functions.

4.4.1 Administrative jurisdiction

Within the administrative branch, the *Conseil d'État* is both an advisory and a judicial body. As the former, it delivers opinions to the Government on legislative and administrative matters and takes part in the law-making process. As a judicial body, it deals with disputes between the administration and its citizens. It may act as a first instance court, as an appeal court and as a cassation court. In first instance, it has general jurisdiction on a series of highly important matters related mainly to regional and European elections and to the appointment of public officials. As a court of appeal, it hears matters previously decided upon by other administrative jurisdictions. As a cassation court, it can quash [*casser*] decisions of lower courts on the grounds of lack of competence, procedural improprieties or misinterpretation of the law. On these occasions, it refers the case to a lower court for judgement. It can also decide on the legality of certain acts issued by the Administration.

The *cours administratives d'appel*, which have only judicial powers, decide appeals on matters already decided upon by previous administrative courts. The *tribunaux administratifs* are regional courts that hear cases, subject to further appeal, related to public administrations. As occurs with the *Conseil d'État*, these courts are both advisory and judicial bodies, although their advisory role is very rarely invoked and is limited to regional requests, usually from the *préfets de département*.

The *juridictions administratives spécialisées* were created due to the complexity of some matters which need to be dealt with by specialist judges. Therefore, they hear cases, in first instance, related to pensions, social benefits, and so on.

4.4.2 Ordinary jurisdiction

The *Cour de cassation* is the highest court of the *ordre judiciaire*. Its role is to ensure that the rule of law is observed by inferior courts when interpreting and applying it. This court does not 'judge' as such, since it does not examine the facts of a case. Rather, it considers the legality of decisions taken by lower courts which are referred to it and examines whether the law has been correctly applied to the facts. If it opines that the law has been properly applied to a case by the inferior court known as *cour d'appel*, it rejects the appeal. If, on the contrary, it decides that the law has not been properly applied, it quashes the decision, which is then sent to the same *cour d'appel* it came from or to another *cour d'appel* to be reconsidered.

This appeal court system, common to the civil and criminal jurisdiction, re-examines the cases brought before it and hears appeals against decisions taken in the first instance by a *tribunal d'instance*, a *tribunal de grande instance*, a *tribunal de commerce*, a *conseil de prud'hommes*, a *tribunal paritaire des baux ruraux*, a *tribunal des affaires de sécurité sociale*, a *tribunal de police* or a *tribunal correctionnel*, as explained below.

The ordinary courts deal with civil and criminal matters. Strictly speaking, separate civil and criminal courts exist, but these are courtrooms that depend on their civil counterparts. The competence of civil courts is based on the principle of adequacy, by which every matter is judged by the most competent judge. Therefore, several civil courts exist depending on the matter to be dealt with, and they can generally be divided into two main categories: general and specialized courts. Within the general courts we find the *tribunal de grande instance*, a collegiate court, and the single judge *tribunal d'instance*. Apart from their composition, the difference between them lies in the nature of the case (some civil matters correspond exclusively to the *tribunal de grande instance* whilst others are judged by the *tribunal d'instance*) and in the amount of money involved in the litigation.

Along with the general courts, there are four specialized courts:

1. The *tribunaux de commerce* are commercial courts competent to try disputes between tradesmen and between individuals concerning commercial transactions. They can also deal with disputes between partners on matters related to the creation, operation or liquidation of a business, or with defaults of payment when the debtor is a trader or a craftsman.
2. The *conseils de prud'hommes* are industrial tribunals with competence to conciliate or to adjudicate on individual employment disputes.

3. The *tribunal des affaires de sécurité sociale* hears social security disputes in first instance, such as social security registration, benefit entitlement or contributions.
4. The *tribunaux paritaires des baux ruraux* are agricultural land tribunals, whose remit is to try disputes between landlords and tenants.

The criminal justice system (*juridictions pénales* or *juridictions répressives*) has a unique structure as a result of a three-stage proceeding. These stages are the pre-trial stage, divided into the prosecution stage, *poursuite*; the investigation, *instruction*, and the trial stage or *jugement*. The trial stage can be followed at three different courts, which are, strictly speaking, the same as the civil courts, named differently when dealing with criminal matters. The criminal courts hear cases depending on the category of the offence: the *tribunal de police* is the lowest and deals with minor offences, specifically with *contraventions de 5ème classe*, which are those minor offences punishable by the highest penalties; the *tribunal correctionnel* is competent to try *délits*, that is, major offences, committed within its territorial jurisdiction. Finally, the *cour d'assises*, consisting not only of professional judges but also of a jury of six (first instance) or nine (appeal) lay people, is competent to try *crimes*, major offences or serious crimes (except those committed by minors, high treason by the President of the Republic and crimes committed by ministers) and offences connected with serious crimes. First instance judgements from the *cour d'assises* cannot be brought to appeal before the *cour d'appel* but to another *cour d'assises* with a different composition. Those pronounced on appeal by a second *cour d'assises* can be appealed in the form of a *pourvoi en cassation* to the *Cour de cassation*.

There are also specialized criminal courts, with a limited jurisdiction based on the personality of the offender (minors, members of Government, the President of the Republic) or on the nature of the offence:

1. The *cours d'assises spéciales*, without a jury, for crimes committed against state security, for military crimes or for crimes against public order, among others.
2. *Juridictions pour mineurs*, amid which the *juge des enfants*, the *tribunal des enfants* and the *cours d'assises des mineurs* are the most important

ones. The differences between them lie mainly in the type of offence committed and the age of the offender.

3. *Juridictions militaires*, for offences committed by members of the armed forces.

4. *Tribunaux maritimes commerciaux*, competent to try maritime offences.

5. The *Haute Cour de Justice*, competent to try the President of the Republic if s/he is suspected of having committed the crime of high treason.

6. The *Cour de Justice de la République*, competent to try members of the Government.

The *juges de proximité* were created by the *loi d'orientation et de programmation sur la justice* of 9 September 2002 and modified by another act of 26 February 2003, with the aim of relieving the work of the *tribunaux d'instance*. The *juges de proximité* have competence both in civil and criminal matters. Their competence in the civil sphere is determined by the nature of the case and by the financial amount involved in the litigation. In criminal matters, they can deal with the *contraventions* of the first four classes, minor offences punishable with the lowest penalties. They can also sit as legal advisers at the *tribunal correctionnel*. Their life, however, has been short as another statute from 13 December 2011, due to come into force on 1 January 2017, has foreseen their gradual disappearance. It is, however, stipulated that their function will subsist and they will be able to develop their functions either at the *tribunaux d'instance* or at the *tribunaux de grande instance*.

4.4.3 Other courts

Apart from the courts just mentioned, there are some other courts which deal with specific matters and can be divided into two main categories: financial courts, the *Cour de comptes*, with administrative and judicial functions, and the *Cour de discipline budgétaire et financière*, competent to impose sanctions for irregularities committed by officials involved in the implementation of the Government budget; and disciplinary courts, sanctioning disciplinary irregularities committed by members of public institutions, the main ones being the *Conseil supérieur de la magistrature*, in charge of guaranteeing the independence of the judges from the executive, the *conseils universitaires*, the *juridictions professionnelles* and the *Autorité de contrôle prudentiel*.

Finally, the *Conseil constitutionnel* is not a supreme court with judicial functions but a jurisdiction embedded with different competences among which the most important one is to control the adherence of the legislation to the Constitution.

4.5 The legal professions in France

There is a wide range of legal careers in France, from lawyers to legal consultants and from judges to judicial and auxiliary personnel. Members of the legal professions can be divided into two distinct categories: *magistrats*, who administer justice, and *auxiliaires de justice*, who assist the *magistrats* or the parties involved.

4.5.1 The judiciary

The *magistrats* are divided into two different groups, depending on whether they judge or they prosecute. The former are called *magistrats du siège* or *magistrats assis* because they perform their functions whilst they are seated, whereas the latter are called *magistrats du parquet* or *magistrats debout* and are part of the *ministère public*. The *magistrats du siège* or *magistrats assis* pass judgements after they have examined a case and have heard the parties and their lawyers. They perform different functions, depending on the matters under discussion, the court they are allocated to and the stage of the proceedings. The following are some examples of *magistrats du siège*:

1. the *juge aux affaires familiales* in the *tribunal de grande instance*, specialized in divorce proceedings;
2. the *juge des enfants*, within the same court, is in charge of questions related to minors in the civil area; and
3. the *juge des tutelles*, in the *tribunal d'instance*, deals with guardianship affairs.

The *magistrats du parquet*, who form the *ministère public*, are responsible for conducting criminal proceedings for serious offences, but they also play an important role representing the interests of society in civil matters. The members of the *ministère public* are answerable to the Government and, according to the principle of separation of judicial functions, they are independent of the *magistrats du siège* and are free to submit opinions to the court. The *magistrats du parquet* are also divided into different categories, depending mainly on their rank, but also on the court where they perform their functions. Thus, the *procureurs*, of a higher rank, share their functions with the *avocats généraux* who are not lawyers, contrary to what their name may suggest, but *magistrats du parquet*, and with the *substituts*, who, having again a name that could suggest a different function, do not replace anyone and are also part of the *ministère public*. The head of the *ministère public* at the *tribunal de grande instance* is called the *Procureur de la République*, whilst the counterpart at the *cour d'appel* and at the *Cour de cassation* is called *Procureur Général*. The *avocats généraux* represent the *ministère public* at the *Cour de cassation, Cour de comptes, cours d'appel* and *cours d'assises* and the *substituts*, of a lower rank, have competences mainly in criminal matters, directly attributed to them by the *Procureur de la République*.

The *juges de proximité*, explained in Section 4.4 above, are not trained *magistrats* and are recruited from the civil society amongst law practitioners and according to specific criteria determined by law.

The diagram below shows the general division of the *magistrats* within the French legal system (see Figure 2).

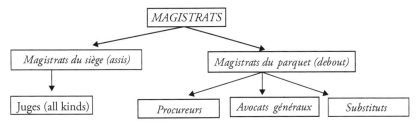

Figure 2: Classification of *magistrats* within the French legal system.

4.5.2 Other legal professions

Another group of professionals involved in the administration of justice are the *auxiliaires de justice*, of which three types can be distinguished: (1) those who assist the parties, particularly the *avocats* and the *avocats aux conseils*, (2) the *officiers ministeriels* such as the *notaire* and the *huissier de justice* and (3) those who assist the judges, *auxiliaires du juge*, among which the *greffiers* and the *police judiciare*.

The *avocats* and the *avocats aux conseils* give advice and assist the parties and represent them during the proceedings. The representation of the parties was traditionally performed by the *avoués* and the *agréés* until they disappeared in 1971 from the lower courts (*tribunal de grande instance* and *tribunaux de commerce*, respectively), and in 2012 the remaining figure of the *avoué* disappeared from the *cour d'appel*, where it still existed. The merger of these two professions into the figure of the *avocat* made the process simpler, it reduced costs for the clients and it harmonized French law with that of other countries.[1] The *avocats* are admitted to the Bar and all those attached to a *tribunal de grande instance* make up a *barreau*, which in turn forms an *ordre*, independent from other orders, with its own legal personality and the aim of promoting the interests of the profession. Every local Bar has a *bâtonnier* as its head.

---

1 However there are some countries belonging to the same Roman tradition where this dual system still exists, as is the case of Spain (see Section 5.5).

The role of the *avocats*, as mentioned before, is of assistance and representation to the parties. They have no territorial restrictions and can plead before any court, whatever its nature (civil, criminal, administrative or disciplinary), except for the *Conseil d'État* and the *Cour de cassation*, where their colleagues, the *avocats aux conseils*, are the only ones authorized to act, and for those courts where the representation of an *avocat* is not necessary. The *avocats aux conseils* are attached to the higher courts, i.e. the *Conseil d'État* and the *Cour de cassation*. Their status is that of *officiers ministériels*, professionals who enjoy the privilege of performing a particular activity generally considered of public interest.

The *officiers ministériels* are those who, whilst not civil servants, have been granted a function for life by the Government, and they enjoy the monopoly of it. In addition to the *avocats aux conseils*, discussed in the previous paragraph, there are two other professions of *officiers ministériels*: the *notaires* and the *huissiers de justice*. The main function of the *notaires*, a profession originating under Roman law, is to draft legal documents which are to be regarded as authentic and enforceable. They do this at the request of the clients. Documents drafted by the *notaires* are usually under the sphere of civil or commercial law and deal with sales of real property, wills, mortgages or settlement of the economic regime of a marriage, amongst others. The *huissiers de justice* perform their duties at the request of individuals or of a judge. They perform a wide range of functions from sending notifications and summons to enforcing court orders and judgements. They also work at the courts, as *huissiers audienciers*, to call the cases and maintain order in the court.

The *auxiliaires du juge* can be grouped into two different categories: the *greffiers* and the *police judiciaire*. The former assist the judge and are responsible for authenticating the acts of the judges and keeping the records of the proceedings. Depending on the court they are attached to, they can also fulfil more specific functions. For instance, in the *tribunaux de grande instance*, the *greffier en chef*, i.e. the head of the *greffe*, who is assisted by the *greffiers*, must keep a copy of the register of births, marriages and deaths, update criminal records, and keep the register of judgements related to the capacity of persons. Finally, the *police judiciaire* conducts investigations under the supervision of the judge or the prosecutor.

CHAPTER 5

Spain

Spanish law has been influenced by many different historical sources and by the rapid evolution of its society over the last fifty years or so. This has shaped a legal system that, even if it owes its essence to Roman law and was deeply influenced by the Napoleonic code, differs greatly from the legal sources from which it originated.

5.1 Historical evolution of the Spanish legal system

Spanish law has been historically influenced by different factors that have played various roles throughout its history and that have merged to produce the existing law, whose main objective is to regulate the social life of the people. When describing the legal history of Spain it is necessary to take into account its social and political dimensions, bearing in mind that over the centuries the territory of Spain has been far larger than its current frontiers. The Spanish American territories, the Philippines, Sardinia, Naples, the Roussillon, The Netherlands or the German Empire, among others, have been part of Spain at some point in history.

The main legal cultures that have influenced the Spanish legal system are the Germanic one and, particularly, Roman law. Canon law, feudal law in a large part of the Iberian Peninsula, Muslim law in topics not related to religion, Jewish law, maritime commercial law and French law, the latter particularly during the nineteenth century, have all played an important role in the evolution of Spanish law (Fernández 1989: 31).

It is possible to differentiate several historical periods in the development of Spanish law from its origins until the present day. The first period corresponds to pre-Roman law, when there were local customary laws ruling the lives of the peoples living in primitive Spain. Little is known about these peoples, although it is thought that they were Celts or Iberians. Primitive laws are thought to have been personal laws, applicable only to the family or local group. When in contact with other groups, the tribes organized agreements called *pactos de hospitalidad* which regulated the relationships between people belonging to different groups (Pérez Prendes 1974: 183–204; Merino Blanco 1996: 1).

The second period coincides with the reception of Roman law in Spain, which was not the same in all territories and varied according to the resistance offered by the different tribes. Society became urbanized and administrative and political life was organized around the urbs, but Roman law – *ius civile* – was only applied to Roman citizens until the year 212, when Emperor Caracalla granted Roman citizenship to all the inhabitants of the Empire, except for the slaves. However, some pre-Roman laws continued to be enforced in some places and local customs were adapted to the circumstances and needs of each area, which meant that Roman law was not applied to the whole territory of Hispania.

At the time of the fall of the Roman Empire, Hispania had already suffered the invasion of several barbarian tribes, which were repelled by the Roman Emperors with the help of another barbarian tribe, the Visigoths, who had already settled in other parts of the Empire, such as France, and who were highly influenced by Rome (Merino Blanco 1996: 4). The Visigoths were, however, not numerous and it is not clear whether they mixed with the Hispanic population. They did not extend throughout the Hispanic territory and established their capital in Toledo. The Visigoths enacted their own laws and codes, although, in some cases, with strong references to and influence from Roman law. Local customs were respected in the matters not covered by the Visigoth laws.

In the year 711 the Visigoths were defeated in the battle of Guadalete, marking the beginning of the Muslim period in Spain, which was to last for eight centuries. The Hispano-Roman population kept their religions, laws, customs and property and some converted to Islam, thus becoming

subject to Muslim law. Some Visigoth laws and codes survived and different laws were applied to different populations and religions: Jews, Muslims
and Christians.

From the eighth to the thirteenth century the law became local,
expressed after the eleventh century by means of the *fueros municipales*.[1]
Little legislation was created and only in those areas where the existing
Visigoth laws and codes were not applicable because there was no solution
to the particular problem. The resistance of the Visigoths and Christians
against the Muslims, known as the *Reconquista*, led to the fragmentation
of the system, with different laws applied in the cities and in rural areas.
Special laws – *fueros* – were passed in those territories reconquered to the
Muslims in order to encourage Christian settlements and in the tenth century the King of León and the Count of Catalonia started to legislate with
general applicability on the whole territory under their control (Merino
Blanco 1996: 6).

During the Middle Ages, a common law – *ius commune* – for all the
Roman Empire was instigated. This common law, created by lawyers (scholars) who integrated their work as well as Roman law and canon law, was
received in France in a generally uniform manner. In Spain, however, the
process was less homogeneous and the different territories accepted the *ius
commune* in varying degrees, giving rise to the emergence of local – *foral* –
laws, which still exist in Spain for some civil aspects.

During the sixteenth and seventeenth centuries, the main characteristic of the Spanish legal system was the increasing powers of the King and
the growing volume of legislation. This, together with the coexistence of
different legal systems in Spain at the time and the need for unity derived
from a unitary Crown, led, at the time of the Spanish War of Succession
after the death of King Carlos III in 1788 and the triumph of Felipe V, to
the abolition of most local laws and the unification of civil law in Spain,
although some aspects remained legislated by *foral* laws.

The spirit of the Age of Enlightenment and the School of Natural law
led to the birth of three new principles in a new conception of the world:

---

1   Legislation regulating local life and establishing norms and rights applicable to the
     local population.

legality, according to which the universe and human nature are subject to laws; rationality, by which the laws governing humanity are derived from the natural laws by the use of reason; and nationality, which recognizes the differences between nations and according to which positive law must be adapted to the circumstances of each nation. These philosophical and political ideas were the catalyst of two major trends in legal history: the creation of state law and the enactment of Constitutions and the codification of law (Merino Blanco 1996: 15). These new ideas also affected Spain and symbolized the origin of the current period of legal history in Spain: the Constitutional period.

Recent legal history in Spain has been marked by the transition period that followed the death of Francisco Franco, the dictator who ruled the country after the Civil War (1936–1939), and the instauration of Democracy. The key moment of this period was the approval of the Spanish Constitution by national referendum on 6 December 1978. Today's Spain is a parliamentary monarchy with the King as the Head of State and the President of the Executive as the Head of the Government. Division of powers exists between the legislative, the executive and the judiciary. Different governments have alternated in the executive since 1977, date of the first democratic elections, and the country has rapidly evolved to accommodate its pace to that of other modern countries in Europe and in the World.

5.2 Organization of law

The main feature in the organization of Spanish law is the internal division between public and private law, as occurs in all legal systems derived from Roman law. Public law refers to the relationships that get established between the Government and the governed. Private law, on the other hand, relates to matters arising among individuals, no matter whether they are citizens or corporate bodies/legal entities. Even if its aim is to protect the common interests of society, this is done through the

protection of private interests. Therefore, public law norms are impera-
tive, as they entail subordination from the citizens, whilst private law
norms require the willingness of the parties, for instance, to marry or
to sign a contract.

The traditional and major areas of public law in Spain, as in other civil
law countries, are constitutional law, administrative law, financial law and
criminal law. As for private law, it mainly covers commercial law, business
law, labour law, and civil law, understood as the regulation of the private
relationships between individuals.

In civil matters, it is important to remember the difference that exists
between the law common to the whole country and the *foral* laws applied
in some Spanish territories, which is due to historical reasons and the
uneven reception of the *ius commune* in the country. As a result, territories
such as Catalonia, Navarre or the Basque Country still apply *foral* laws,
i.e. former local customary laws, in some civil areas such as inheritance or
aspects of family law.

5.3 Sources of law in Spain

As in any other legal system inspired by Roman law, the supreme law of
the Spanish legal system is the law enacted by parliament. Article 1.1. of
the Spanish civil code establishes that the sources of the Spanish legal
system are legislation, customary law and the general principles of law,
whilst article 6 of the same code states that case law complements the
legal system with the legal doctrine established by the Spanish Supreme
Court when interpreting and applying legislation, customary law and
the general principles of law.

Legislation is then the primary, almost exclusive, source of the
Spanish legal system. Custom (customary laws) and general principles of
law are considered to be complementary sources, whilst case law (from
the *Tribunal Supremo* and *Tribunal Constitucional*) and legal doctrine

(scholarly writings) are explanatory sources which may guide the judges when applying the law as to the meaning of the primary sources.

International treaties are also a source of law. Article 1.5 of the Spanish civil code establishes that legal rules from international treaties are not applicable in Spain until they have been published in the Spanish Official Gazette. An exception to the rule are the original EC treaties, which have the same hierarchical level as the Spanish Constitution. International treaties are incorporated into the Spanish legal system once they have been duly signed and ratified, without any further action by any state body. Regular international treaties, i.e. all international treaties except the founding ones of the European Communities, have a hierarchical position similar to the Spanish law.

As for the primary sources of law, there are different legislative levels, with the 1978 Constitution, the original EC treaties and the constitutions of the regional governments (*Estatutos de Autonomía de las Comunidades Autónomas*) at the top of this hierarchy. Below these, we can find national laws, EU law and regional laws. Finally, there are sources with legal value such as rules of law that are not derived from parliament but from the Government.

5.3.1 The 1978 Constitution

The Constitution, the supreme law of the Spanish legal system, establishes the fundamental rights and freedoms that structure the legal system and that are the reference for all other norms.

5.3.2 Founding treaties of the EU

Since the entry of Spain into the European Communities in 1986, the original EC treaties are, together with the Constitution and the *Estatutos de Autonomía de las Comunidades Autónomas*, at the first legislative level among the sources of law. As a consequence of Spain being a member state of the former European Communities, now the European Union, derivative legislation enacted by the EU is automatically binding in Spain. In this regard, and as Merino Blanco mentions (1996: 36), the Spanish Supreme Court has reinforced this view in its judgement of 28 April 1987, *Depósitos Francos*, where it states that 'European Community Law has direct effect and supremacy over national law by virtue of the partial cession of sovereignty brought about by the accession to the European Community'.

5.3.3 Estatutos de Autonomía de las Comunidades Autónomas

The 1978 Constitution acknowledged the regional traditions of the country and divided the state into seventeen *comunidades autónomas*, each of them with various degrees of power and governed by the *Estatutos de Autonomía*, regional constitutions which contain the competences assigned to each region or *comunidad autónoma*. The *Estatutos de Autonomía* are situated at the same legislative level as the Constitution and the original EC treaties.

5.3.4 National legislation

There are different types of national legislation: legislation passed by the parliament, rules of law emanating from the Government by special delegation and special powers derived from the Constitution.

The *ley orgánica* is a special type of law established by the Constitution to regulate certain matters, particularly in the areas of fundamental rights and liberties, as stated in article 81 of the Spanish Constitution. *Leyes orgánicas* are subject to a special procedure for their elaboration, approval, modification and derogation. *Leyes ordinarias*, the generic model of laws, are situated at the same level as the *leyes orgánicas*, the difference being that the *leyes ordinarias* legislate on all matters not included in article 81 of the Constitution.

At the second legislative level, together with the *leyes orgánicas* and *leyes ordinarias* just described, we find derivative legislation enacted by the EU, which is automatically binding in Spain, as well as regional legislation enacted by the *comunidades autónomas*, binding only in the region where it has been enacted.

Due to the high number of issues regulated by parliament and to the lengthy procedure for the approval of organic and ordinary laws, articles 82 to 86 of the Spanish Constitution allow for some matters to be regulated by the Government, under the names of *decretos leyes* and *decretos legislativos*. Article 86 states that, in cases of urgency and extreme need, the Government can introduce regulations which have legal force. However, the Constitution imposes some limits to this power and a *decreto-ley* may not impact on the organization of the basic institutions of the state or of the *comunidades autónomas*, the civil rights and liberties contained in Title I of the Constitution or the general electoral regime. In addition, the *decreto-ley* needs to be submitted to the parliament for approval and ratification within a 30-day period. Once approved, there is a procedure whereby the parliament can convert a *decreto-ley* into an ordinary law. On some occasions, the parliament may decide to delegate its powers to the Government for the regulation of certain matters (article 85 of the Constitution), in which case the legislation enacted by the Government is called a *decreto legislativo*.

At the third legislative level we find all the legislation emanating from the Government and the Public Administration. Depending on the hierarchy between them and the body which enacts them, there are different types of *normas reglamentarias*: *decretos, órdenes, instrucciones* and *circulares*.

5.4 The Spanish court system

Following the principle of unity of jurisdiction, the court system is based on a single jurisdiction. Accordingly, there is a single body of judges and courts are centralized, even if there are different areas of jurisdiction organized on a regional or local basis, on the subject matter, on the cost of the litigation or on their function. Some courts have national competence throughout the country, as is the case of the *Audiencia Nacional,* whilst others have only regional or local competence or jurisdiction, but are still courts of the state. For jurisdictional reasons, Spain is divided into municipalities, *partidos judiciales,*[2] provinces, regions (*comunidades autónomas*) and the whole country.

As for the subject matter, courts are organized around main four areas of law: civil law (in the sense of private personal law, i.e. family, inheritance, property, contracts, etc.), criminal law, administrative law and labour law (including social security law). Some of the ordinary courts have somewhat become specialized, as is the case of the *Juzgados de Violencia sobre la Mujer* (courts dealing with violence against women) or the *Juzgados de Vigilancia Penitenciaria* (courts with special duties in the matter of criminal sentencing). Nonetheless, they are not special courts and remain ordinary courts, as the Spanish legal system excludes the existence of such special courts. The only exception to the unity of jurisdiction and the prohibition of special courts are the military courts, focused on criminal matters under the Spanish military jurisdiction.

It is important to differentiate between one-judge courts and collegiate courts. The former, called *juzgados,* count on *jueces* who judge cases at the first instance. The latter are *tribunales* or *audiencias* and they are made up of three or five members, called *magistrados.* The court system in Spain follows a hierarchical organization with a system of jurisdictional appeals and the courts are organized according to three main criteria: subject matter, territorial competence and hierarchy of courts. Taking the table below as the starting point, we will proceed to analyse the different courts in Spain (see Table 4).

2   Judicial districts include several bordering municipalities belonging to the same province. The main municipality of a *partido judicial* is called *cabeza de partido.*

Table 4: Composition, territorial competence, subject matter and instance of the
Spanish courts

	Composition	Territorial competence	Subject matter	Instance
Tribunal Supremo	Collegiate	Whole country	All subject matters: civil, criminal, labour, administrative and military.	Appeal
Audiencia Nacional	Collegiate	Whole country	Administrative, criminal and labour (special matters)	Only instance
Tribunal Superior de Justicia	Collegiate	Regional (*comunidad autónoma*)	Civil, criminal, administrative, labour	Appeal / First instance (depending on the subject matter)
Audiencia Provincial	Collegiate	Province	Civil and criminal	Appeal
Juzgado de Primera Instancia e Instrucción	One-judge	Main municipality of the *partido judicial*	Civil and criminal	First instance (civil) and investigation (criminal)
Juzgado de lo Penal	One-judge	Province	Criminal	First instance
Juzgado de lo Contencioso-Administrativo	One-judge	Province	Administrative	First or only instance
Juzgado de lo Social	One-judge	Province	Labour and Social Security	First instance
Juzgado de Vigilancia Penitenciaria	One-judge	Province	Criminal	First instance
Juzgado de lo Mercantil	One-judge	Province	Commercial, Company	First instance
Juzgado de Menores	One-judge	Province	Criminal	First instance

	Composition	Territorial competence	Subject matter	Instance
Juzgado de Violencia Sobre la Mujer	One-judge	Province	Criminal	First instance
Juzgado de Paz	One-judge	Each of the secondary municipalities of the *partido judicial*	Civil and criminal	First instance

The *Tribunal Supremo*, a collegiate court with supreme jurisdiction over the whole of Spain, is divided into five different chambers or *salas* which judge cases according to the subject matter: civil, criminal, administrative, labour and military. It hears cases on appeal and in cassation.

The *Audiencia Nacional* is a collegiate court with jurisdiction in administrative, criminal and labour cases for the whole country. The particularity of this court is that there are specific areas reserved to it in the first instance, such as crimes against the Crown or the government, counterfeit or monetary crimes, and terrorism, among others. It also hears cases on appeal.

The *Tribunales Superiores de Justicia* are collegiate courts with civil, criminal, labour and administrative jurisdiction over the territory of the region where they have their seat. They hear cases both on first instance and on appeal.

The *Audiencias Provinciales* are collegiate courts with competence to hear civil and criminal cases within the territory of a province. On civil matters they hear cases on appeal from the *Juzgados de Primera Instancia* from the province. On criminal matters they have first instance jurisdiction on serious crimes, but they also hear cases on appeal from the *Juzgados de lo Penal, Juzgados de Instrucción* and *Juzgados de Menores*.

The rest are all single judge courts. The *Juzgados de Primera Instancia e Instrucción* have civil and criminal jurisdiction in the territory of a *partido judicial*. These courts hear civil cases in first instance and conduct the preliminary investigations in criminal cases that will be then judged in a *Juzgado de lo Penal*. In practice, these courts also hear some cases on appeal and decide some criminal cases. The *Juzgados de lo Penal* hear criminal cases at first instance within the jurisdiction of a province, whereas the *Juzgados de lo Contencioso-Administrativo* hear cases involving the administration.

The *Juzgados de lo Social* have jurisdiction in the province where they have their seat, regarding labour law or social security matters. The *Juzgados de Vigilancia Penitenciaria* have jurisdiction in the province and their function is to enforce criminal judgements which foresee imprisonment and other security measures. They also safeguard the rights of those imprisoned. The *Juzgados de lo Mercantil* deal with insolvency proceedings and other commercial matters.

The *Juzgados de Menores* are juvenile courts which judge criminal offences committed by minors and the supervision of educational measures imposed on them, whilst the *Juzgados de Violencia sobre la Mujer* are ordinary courts specialized in hearing cases involving domestic violence. The *Juzgados de Paz*, run by non-professional judges, are located in municipalities which do not have a *Juzgado de Primera Instancia e Instrucción*, and they hear minor cases on civil and criminal matters.

Apart from the courts just described and as happens in France, there is a Spanish court which strictly speaking does not belong to the court system as such but it is only subject to the Constitution: the *Tribunal Constitucional*. Its main function is to interpret the Constitution, by supervising and monitoring the legislation approved by the Parliament to ensure it is not contrary to the Constitution. It also controls the activities of the executive and the judiciary. Other courts are the *Tribunal de Cuentas*, responsible for controlling public accounts and auditing political parties or the courts belonging to the military jurisdiction, a special jurisdiction for members of the armed forces. The *Tribunal del Jurado*, not a court itself but a jury formed by lay citizens, is called to judge certain crimes as specified in the legislation.

5.5 The legal professions in Spain

The figure below summarizes the organization of the legal professions in the Spanish Administration of Justice, the official section within the state which enforces and ensures the application of law (see Figure 3).

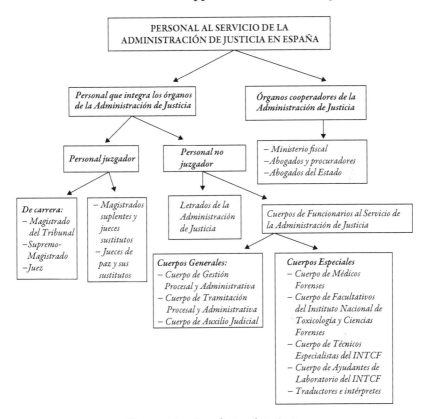

Figure 3: Legal professionals in Spain.

5.5.1 The judiciary

The professionals of the Administration of Justice (the official section within the state which applies and ensures the application of law) can be divided into the judiciary and other personnel. The former group is made up of permanent members who have passed a selective examination and hold their post for life, among whom we find the ordinary judges working at the *juzgados*, the *magistrados* of the *tribunal* or *audiencia*, and the *magistrados del Tribunal Supremo*. As mentioned before, the *jueces de paz* are non-professional or lay judges holding their post at the *Juzgados de Paz*. Together with these members of the judiciary, all of whom must pass a competitive selection procedure (except for the *jueces de paz*) there are also temporary judges who are not members of the judiciary, but who can perform judicial functions in some circumstances, such as holding office when a permanent judge cannot be appointed. Generally speaking, all members of the judiciary are called judges, notwithstanding the judicial body to which they belong or the functions performed. Members of the judiciary are subject to a strict regime of incompatibilities in order to guarantee their independence in the enforcement of the law. They can only be dismissed, transferred, suspended or forced to retire in accordance with the terms provided by law.

5.5.2 Other legal professions

Besides the judiciary there are other members of the Administration of Justice who do not judge, but whose work is essential for the application of law. The *Letrados de la Administración de Justicia*, formerly *Secretarios Judiciales*, run the courts, organize the proceedings and assist the judges by keeping the documents and records of the judicial activities in the court. They also guarantee the smooth running of proceedings. The other group are the *Cuerpos de Funcionarios al servicio de la Administración de Justicia*, subdivided into two more wide groups where different categories exist. The *Cuerpos Generales* were established in 2002 to replace the former *oficiales*, *auxiliares* and *agentes*, and are responsible for the administrative tasks and the day to day running of the courts or agencies to which they are attached. The *Cuerpos Especiales* from different disciplines, either civil servants or independent experts, assist the courts in administering justice. Among these, the translators and interpreters provide official translations of documents and interpreting services during the proceedings, among other tasks.

Other categories cooperate with these professionals in rendering the law: *fiscales, abogados, procuradores, policía judicial* and *abogados del Estado*.

According to article 124 of the Spanish Constitution, the *fiscales* are members of the *Fiscalía* or *Ministerio Fiscal* responsible for prosecuting and for the application of justice by defending the rights of the citizens, protecting the public interest and safeguarding the independence of the courts. They must pass a competitive examination to hold a post and their hierarchy and remuneration are similar to those of the judges. They are also subject to the same civil and criminal liability and have the same rights of independence and irremovability.

The defence of the parties must be performed jointly by an *abogado* and a *procurador*. The former is a member of an independent profession focused on the advice, conciliation and defence of public and private interests. The *abogados* are the only ones who can perform the legal defence of the parties, are organized in professional associations called *Colegios de abogados* and must belong to one of them to be able to practice the profession. The *procuradores*, just like the *abogados*, are lawyers but the difference between them is that the latter perform the legal defence of the parties, whilst the former, the *procuradores*, are the only ones entitled to represent the parties in court through a power of attorney given by the client. Both professionals must work together as the participation of *procuradores* is compulsory in most civil proceedings and in all criminal ones. Usually, clients approach *abogados* for advice and these appoint a *procurador* who represent the client in court. The *procuradores* are also organized in professional associations called *Colegios de procuradores*.

The *abogados del Estado* represent and defend the state and its public bodies, although on some special occasions it is also possible to leave the legal defence of the state in the hands of a private practitioner. Lawyers

who form part of the *Cuerpo de Letrados del Estado* must pass a competitive examination to join this body. Finally, the *notarios*, or notaries public,
are remnants of the Roman law as in Italy, France and Germany. As public
officials, they must pass a competitive examination and carry out the same
functions described above for their Italian or French counterparts.

CHAPTER 6

Germany

By Rafael Adolfo Zambrana Kuhn

6.1 Historical evolution of the German legal system

The ancient Germanic peoples each had their own customs and practices. In the absence of written law, these played a capital role in the ruling of the community. After the fall of the Roman Empire in the West in the fifth century, Germanic tribes occupied some of its former territories. The new rulers did not try to impose their customs, so that the local population continued applying the existing Roman law, and some elements of the latter were integrated into the old Germanic traditions. The *Edictum Theoderici* is an early compilation dating back to the fifth or sixth centuries and written in Latin. It combined elements of Germanic and Roman law, and had a territorial application, thus it applied to the whole population regardless of their German or Roman origin. During the early Middle Ages the Catholic Church played a major role in the administration of the territory throughout Europe. So it started compiling its own written canon law, dealing with matters such as betrothal, marriage, testament or patronage.

Around the twelfth century, old Germanic oral traditions and customary law were laid down in compilations. One such piece of work is the *Sachsenspiegel*, translated from Latin into the vernacular by Eike von Repgow around 1220–1235. It was a combination of both common and feudal law, and became widespread throughout Central and Eastern Europe. Another example is the *Schwabenspiegel*, dated around 1275, which combined elements from the Pentateuch, Roman law and canon law, and was enforced in Southern Germany, Bohemia, Moravia and Silesia. At about this time the prestigious Law Faculty in Bologna, Italy, was undertaking the systematic study of the *Corpus Iuris Civilis* (CIC), the legal compilation issued by order of Byzantine Emperor Justinian (527–565). With the publication of annotated editions, the CIC became known in the rest of Europe. The absence of a central administration in the German territories, the relative weakness of the Imperial Court – which acted merely as an appellate organ – and the lack of a strong body of imperial jurists were three factors which made reception of Roman law easier here than in other European countries such as England or France. However the decisive factor was that Germanic customary law was becoming increasingly ill-suited for the deep social changes occurring at the time. Thus Roman law was enforced in cases where local laws could not offer a satisfactory solution to the problem at hand. Up to this time, judges had been making their decisions 'on the basis of traditional legal knowledge, practical wisdom, experience, and practicality, and from an intuitive perception of [...] the case' (Zweigert and Kötz 1998: 134).

The newly rediscovered corpus allowed for a systematic approach to judicial activity, which enabled a more consistent legal practice. Besides, Roman law was considered a helpful means to establishing the Emperor of the Germans as the legitimate historical successor of the ancient Roman Caesar. German universities began teaching courses in Roman law, the development of which led to the creation of the *Usus Modernus Pandectarum*. This meant a new combination of Roman law and traditional custom, establishing a mutual influence between them. As a result of the Enlightenment, in the seventeenth century, Roman law was rationalized and adapted to the new spirit of the time. Many obsolete concepts and institutions were revised in the new light of reason. The key concept to this process was codification: the notion that all legislation could and should be rationally systematized.

Following the decline of the Holy Roman Empire a large mosaic of national German-speaking states came into being in the late eighteenth century, each one with its particular political structure. These were extremely variegated, ranging from monarchies to duchies or even free cities, just to mention a few. Each one of them also had its own particular legislation. Thus, for instance, Prussian law still maintained some of the nobility's traditional privileges, whereas Baden adopted the French *code civil* with its modern principles of equality and freedom of property.

Throughout the nineteenth century there were several attempts to bring these various states together into a national entity. The first attempt was to create a rather loose confederation (*Deutscher Bund*, 1815–1866). Rivalry between Austria and Prussia gave rise to tensions which finally led to war. After Austria's defeat and exclusion a new federation (*Norddeutscher Bund*, 1867–1870) came into being. A Constitution was drafted and approved. Without the presence of Austria, which had so far been the leading power, the new federal state came strongly under the influence of the Prussian monarchy. These changes eventually led to war with France, but finally, after the Prussian victory in 1870–1871, the constellation of territories united to form the German Empire. King Wilhelm I of Prussia was proclaimed Kaiser in the Hall of Mirrors at the Palace of Versailles.

A new code of civil law, the *Bürgerliches Gesetzbuch* (*BGB*) was drafted and, after a very long and complicated process, finally approved in 1896. It came into effect on 1 January 1900. The general phrasing used in some of its clauses, for instance §242, rendered a flexible code that could be adapted to new situations. This would prove to be a very important asset, for example after the First and the Second World Wars. In 1949 the creation of the Federal Republic (FRG) and the Democratic Republic (GDR) gave way to a division in the political and legal systems. In the FRG the inclusion of the fundamental rights in the constitutional text, the *Grundgesetz* (GG), helped extend the longevity of the BGB. Since all present and future legislation would have to be bound by the GG, all legal provisions would have to be interpreted or adapted accordingly. Of course the BGB was eventually subject to modifications, and sometimes extended through new legislation. But most of it stayed in force until the year 2000. At this time it underwent its first thorough revision, mainly in order to adapt it to the considerable amount of EU legislation passed in the meantime.

The Constitution, *Verfassung*, of the former German Democratic Republic, strongly influenced by the USSR, also stated a number of fundamental rights, at least formally, but there was no private property, no separation of powers, and whatever individual liberty there might be it was basically submitted to the needs of the state. A socialist political system was established and East Berlin became the capital of the GDR. We will not expand on former GDR law here, since it does not really relate to Western European legal systems.

Initially the *Grundgesetz* was approved by and for the Federal Republic. It was meant to be provisional, hence the avoidance of the more formal title *Verfassung*, until the time came when the German people would reunite, and free elections could take place in the whole country. After the collapse of the German Democratic Republic in 1989, its former territory was divided into five new *Länder*: Brandenburg, Mecklenburg-Western Pomerania, Saxony, Saxony-Anhalt and Thuringia. These were integrated into the Federal Republic, along with the previously existing *Länder*: Baden-Württemberg, Bavaria, Bremen, Hamburg, Hesse, Lower Saxony, North Rhine-Westphalia, Rhineland-Palatinate, Saarland and Schleswig-Holstein. The city of Berlin, which had so far had a special status, was reunified, granted the same status as the other fifteen *Länder* and became the new capital of the Federal Republic. A constitutional reform was not deemed necessary and the *Grundgesetz* is now in effect in the whole national territory. However a transition period was established – for some specific issues extending as far as 2015 – in order to allow the new *Länder* to smoothly adapt their previous legal system to that of the Federal Republic. The *Grundgesetz* was last modified in 2006.

6.2 Organization of law

Like other legal systems based on ancient Roman law, the German legal system distinguishes public from private law. The latter regulates the relationship between citizens or groups of citizens, i.e. subjects of law on a same level, establishing their rights and obligations. Public law deals, on the one hand, with the relationship between the citizens and the state, the holder of public power. On the other hand, it also governs the relationship between different instances of the said power, i.e. between the Federation and the *Länder*.

We must bear in mind the autonomy enjoyed by the *Länder* when legislating within their policy areas. Some matters are exclusively regulated by federal law, while others are shared with or even left totally to the *Länder*. In spite of the restrictions imposed upon it, the legislative competence of the *Länder* is explicitly safeguarded in art. 79(3) of the *Grundgesetz*. In 2006 the *Grundgesetz* was deeply reformed and, as a result, legislative competences of both the Federation and the *Länder* were redistributed, allowing the latter to play a greater role in the enforcement of the law.

We have already mentioned the inclusion of some fundamental principles in the tenor of the *Grundgesetz*. Amongst these we can mention, for example:

- inviolability of human dignity and its defence through the powers of the state (art. 1 (1));
- recognition of the inviolable and inalienable human rights (art. 1 (2));
- submission of the powers of the state to basic rights (art. 1 (3));
- republican and democratic government under the rule of law (art. 20 (1); art. 28 (1));
- sovereignty of the people (art. 20 (2));
- exercise of power by the people through election of their representatives and through the organs of the legislative, executive and judicial powers (art. 20 (2));
- submission of all legislation to the Constitution; submission of the executive and the judicial powers to law and statute (art. 20 (3)).

These principles were introduced as a future safeguard against the dangerous consequences derived from an unstable system, as the Republic of Weimar had been, or even a dictatorial regime, such as the Third Reich.

The *Strafgesetzbuch* (StGB), code of criminal law, dates back to 1871. The 1998 version, although with some later modifications, is still in force today. The StGB is the core of German criminal law and consists of a general part and a particular part. The former (*allgemeiner Teil*) deals with general notions on punishable acts and their legal consequences. The particular part (*besonderer Teil*) describes the full array of specific offences and establishes their corresponding punishment. Together with the StGB, there are other legal texts which also contain dispositions on criminal matters. In this way it is possible to develop criminal law and to adapt it to modern circumstances, for example regarding environmental protection.

The legal texts we have mentioned so far are some examples of what is known as substantive law. But there are also compilations of procedural law regulating the process in which substantive law must be applied. Two very important examples of the latter are the *Zivilprozessordnung* (ZPO), code of civil procedure, and the *Strafprozessordnung* (StPO), code of criminal procedure. A detailed analysis would by far exceed the scope of this work, so suffice here to present an overview of these two codes. We will be following the translation provided by Von Schöning (<www.gesetze-im-internet. de/englisch_zpo/index.html>).

In addition to regulating all aspects of compulsory enforcement of court decisions, *Zwangsvollstreckung*, the ZPO also regulates those matters concerning contentious proceedings in civil law such as:

- Jurisdiction, parties, costs of proceedings, etc.
- First instance and appellate remedies: appeal, appeal on points of law, complaints.
- Reopening of proceedings: annulment, retrial.
- Summary procedure based on documentary evidence or related to a bill of exchange.
- Summary proceedings for a payment order.

Finally the ZPO deals with matters like:

- Arbitration proceedings.
- Judicial collaboration within the EU.

The StPO deals basically with the following matters:

- General provisions: on matters like jurisdiction, venue, participants, court decisions, notifications, witnesses, experts, detention, examining of the accused, defence counsel, etc.
- The first instance: indictment, prosecution, proceedings, main hearing, etc.

- Appellate remedies: complaint, appeal, cassation.
- Reopening of proceedings concluded by a final judgment.
- Participation of the aggrieved person in the proceedings: private prosecution, accessory prosecution, compensation for the aggrieved person, etc.
- Rights of the aggrieved person.
- Special types of procedure: procedure for criminal orders, procedure for preventive detention, accelerated procedure, procedure concerning confiscation and seizure of property, procedure for imposing regulatory fines.
- Execution of sentence and costs of proceedings.
- Provision of information and inspection of files, use of information, provisions on data files, etc.

We have already discussed the code of civil law (BGB), which constitutes the core of German private law. Along with the BGB mention must be made of the *Handelsgesetzbuch* (HGB), commercial code; the *GmbH-Gesetz* (GmbHG), Limited Liability Company Act, and the *Aktiengesetz* (AktG), Stock Corporation Act. While the BGB applies to all citizens, the latter only affect those individuals and institutions (corporations) engaged professionally in business and commerce. They are truly essential for the modern social market economy, which can only prosper on the basis of legal security.

6.3 Sources of law in Germany

Sources of law can be divided into primary and secondary sources.

6.3.1 *Primary sources*

Gesetz is passed by the organs of the legislative power – the federal parliament (*Bundestag*) and the Council of the *Länder* (*Bundesrat*) – and sanctioned by the President of the Republic. It represents the main source of law.

Rechtsverordnung are legal texts passed by the executive and are also an important source of law. They require authorization by the legislative regarding their contents, objectives and extent. Hard restrictions apply in order to ensure that the principle of separation of powers prevails.

Satzungen are approved by different bodies of public or private law in their areas of competence, according to the principle of self-administration. However the capacity of such bodies has to be established by law.

Gewohnheitsrecht, the oldest source of law, refers to common practices which were traditionally accepted and expected in the community, later often adopted into written law.

6.3.2 Secondary sources

Secondary sources of law include general principles of law and case law. General principles of law are generally accepted as a subsidiary source: *pacta sunt servanda*, i.e. obligations must be met; *nulla poena sine culpa*, i.e. no punishment without guilt; *nullum crimen sine lege*, i.e. no crime without law; *in dubio pro reo*, i.e. when in doubt [decide] in favour of the defendant. Strictly speaking, case precedents are not as binding as they are in the Anglo-Saxon legal system. Therefore court rulings are not considered by all experts as a proper source of German law. Basically, in Germany the instances of the judiciary are rather independent from one another, but all constitutional organs and authorities are bound by certain decisions of the *Bundesverfassungsgericht* (*BVG*). Furthermore, when there are concurring decisions by the *Bundesgerichtshof* (*BGH*) and the *Oberlandesgerichte* (*OLG*) on some specific matter, then these decisions are also usually adopted into the legislation. In such cases there is no doubt about them being proper sources of law.

6.3.3 International sources of law

Similar to what happens in other European countries (see Chapter 3) the international sources of law in Germany consist of bilateral and multilateral treaties and agreements, together with European Union law. International treaties must be approved or ratified by the German government and published in the *Bundesgesetzblatt* before coming into force. Some international treaties can be directly enforced, while some others may require a previous national transposition.

European Union law

As in all other member states, EU legislation is an important source of law in Germany. EU law consists of primary legislation (treaties establishing the EU), secondary legislation (directives, regulations and decisions) and supplementary law (including case law, international law and general principles of EU law). While directives and regulations affect all member states, decisions are only binding on those to whom they are addressed. Recommendations and opinions have no binding force.

6.4 The German court system

The Judicial power is entrusted to the *Richter*, whose status and activity is basically regulated by the *Deutsches Richtergesetz* (DRiG). They can be appointed for life or temporarily. Only professional judges can intervene within the ordinary jurisdiction in civil and family law hearings, and they usually act on their own (*Einzelrichter*). Under certain circumstances, for example if there is no prosecutor available or if there is urgency, criminal cases can be investigated by a prosecuting judge (*Ermittlungsrichter*). The hearings will then be held in a different court, which can consist of one or more professional judges (*Strafrichter*) together with two or more citizens appointed as lay judges (*Schöffen*). The figure of the lay judge embodies the constitutional principle of the citizens' taking part in the administration of justice. These citizens are appointed for certain trials (criminal and juvenile hearings, at both local and regional courts) acting on the same level as the professional judge(s). They must decide whether the defendant is guilty and, in that case, what sentence is to be applied. Lay judges are appointed for a period of five years. Not all citizens are eligible, for example they must be over twenty-five and under seventy years old, they cannot have been previously convicted, and certain professionals are excused. However a very powerful reason is necessary to decline, once the appointment has been made. Lay judges have to attend all proceedings and therefore they receive a legally established compensation. They have access to official brochures with all relevant information about the legal system and their task within it.

Apart from the above mentioned, there are also honorary judges, named *ehrenamtlicher Richter*, acting in the commercial divisions of the Regional Courts and in the Administrative, Labour and Social Courts. Honorary judges are usually professionals in their respective fields, appointed because of their specific qualification.

As the table below shows, the German court system is basically structured on three levels (see Table 5). In the ordinary jurisdiction, the first level consists of courts of the first instance, both at local level (*Amtsgericht*, AG) and at regional level (*Landgericht*, LG). The AG deals with civil law hearings when the amount in dispute is up to 5,000 euro, as well as with criminal hearings with prison sentences of up to two years (single judge, *Einzelrichter*) or up to four years (*Schöffengericht*, consisting of one professional judge together with two lay judges). The LG deals with civil law hearings when the amount in dispute is over 5,000 euro and with criminal hearings relating to serious crimes (*große Strafkammer*, consisting of three professional and two lay judges) or capital offences (*Schwurgericht*, also consisting of three professional and two lay judges).

The second level consists of appeal courts, the *Berufungsinstanz*. The LG is a revision instance for sentences by the AG both in civil cases and criminal cases (one judge and two lay judges, *kleine Strafkammer*). The *Oberlandesgericht* (OLG) is the second instance for sentences by the LG in civil cases. Basically the appeal can be a material revision (i.e. relating to the legal matter) and/or a formal revision (i.e. relating to the rightful application of the procedures).

In the third level we find the OLG as a cassation court (*Revisionsinstanz*) for sentences by the AG and the LG in criminal cases. There is also the *Bundesgerichtshof* (BGH) as a cassation instance for sentences by the OLG in civil cases, and for sentences by the LG in both civil and criminal hearings. The cassation is exclusively a formal revision and does not deal with the legal matter.

In Bavaria there is a superior instance in the ordinary jurisdiction with no equivalent in other *Länder*: the *Bayerisches Oberstes Landesgericht* (BayObLG), which is the cassation court for civil sentences affecting Bavarian law (instead of the BGH) and also for criminal sentences (instead of the OLG).

Table 5: German court system

Ordinary Jurisdiction	Special Jurisdictions				
Civil / Criminal Jur.	Administrative Jur.	Labour Jur.	Social Jur.	Financial Jur.	Patents Jur.
Bundesgerichtshof Zivilsenat / Strafsenat	*Bundesverwaltungsgericht*	*Bundesarbeitsgericht*	*Bundessozialgericht*	*Bundesfinanzhof* / *Finanzgericht*	*Bundesgerichtshof Patentkammer* / *Bundespatentgericht Beschwerdesenat, Nichtigkeitssenat*
Oberlandesgericht Zivilsenat / Strafsenat	*Bayerisches Oberste Landesgericht (only in Bavaria)* / *Oberverwaltungsgericht*	*Landesarbeitsgericht*	*Landessozialgericht*		
Landgericht Zivilkammer / kleine Strafkammer, große Strafkammer, Schwurgericht	*Verwaltungsgericht*	*Arbeitsgericht*	*Sozialgericht*		
Amtsgericht Richter / Schöffengericht					

Similarly to what happens in the ordinary jurisdiction, in the special jurisdictions the *Oberverwaltungsgericht* (OVerwG), the *Landesarbeitsgericht* (LAG) and the *Landessozialgericht* (LSG) are the respective appellate instances for sentences by the *Verwaltungsgericht* (VerwG), the *Arbeitsgericht* (ArbG) and the *Sozialgericht* (SG). The *Bundesverwaltungsgericht* (BVerwG), the *Bundesarbeitsgericht* (BAG) and the *Bundessozialgericht* (BSG) are the respective cassation instances. In Baden-Württemberg, Bavaria and Hesse the equivalent of the *Oberverwaltungsgericht* is the *Verwaltungsgerichtshof* (VerwGH). As an exception to the three-level structure, the financial and the patents jurisdictions only have two instances, both at federal level.

Those actions that can be implemented against court decisions are called legal remedies. When, how and where these remedies are appropriate is determined by procedural regulations. The figures below show which legal remedies may apply in the different jurisdictions (see Figures 4 and 5).

Civil jurisdiction	AG →	LG →	OLG ⇨	BGH/BayObLG*
	AG	ठठ	OLG	(only for Family law)
Criminal jurisdiction	AG →	LG ⇨	OLG/BayObLG* ⇨ BGH	
	AG	ठठ	OLG	
		LG	⇨ठ	BGH

KEY:
→   Appeal (*Berufung*) (on points of fact and/or law)
⇨   Cassation (*Revision*) (on points of law only)
ठठ   Immediate appeal (*Sprungrevision*) (on points of law only)
*   In Bavaria!

Figure 4: Appellate remedies in the ordinary jurisdiction, Germany.

Administrative jurisdiction	
	VerwG → OVerwG/VerwGH* (⇨ BayObLG**) ⇨ BVerwG
Labour jurisdiction	ArbG → LAG ⇨ BAG
Social jurisdiction	SG → LSG ⇨ BSG
Finance jurisdiction	FG ⇨ BFH
Patents jurisdiction	BPG ⇨ BGH

KEY:
→   Appeal (*Berufung*) (on points of fact and/or law)
⇨   Cassation (Revision) (on points of law only)
*   In Baden-Württemberg, Bavaria and Hesse
**   In Bavaria

Figure 5: Appellate remedies in the special jurisdictions, Germany.

The German Foreign Office (*Auswärtiges Amt*) together with the Federal Ministry of Justice (*Bundesministerium der Justiz*, today *Bundesministerium der Justiz und für Verbraucherschutz*) approved an official translation into English, French and Spanish of all the above mentioned jurisdictional instances, for use by sworn translators and interpreters (Jessnitzer 1982: 52–5), as shown in the table below (see Table 6).

Table 6: Translation of the German courts into English, French and Spanish

Amtsgericht (AG)	Local Court *Tribunal cantonal* *Juzgado Local*
Landgericht (LG)	Regional Court *Tribunal régional* *Tribunal Regional*
Oberlandesgericht (OLG)	Higher Regional Court *Tribunal régional supérieur* *Tribunal Regional Superior*
Bundesgerichtshof (BGH)	Federal Court of Justice *Cour fédérale de Justice* *Corte Federal de Justicia*
Arbeitsgericht (ArbG)	Labour Court *Tribunal du Travail* *Tribunal de Trabajo*
Landesarbeitsgericht (LAG)	Higher Labour Court *Tribunal supérieur du Travail* *Tribunal Superior de Trabajo*
Bundesarbeitsgericht (BAG)	Federal Labour Court *Cour fédérale du Travail* *Corte Federal de Trabajo*
Sozialgericht (SG)	Social Court *Tribunal de contentieux social* *Tribunal de Asuntos de Seguridad Social*
Landessozialgericht (LSG)	Higher Social Court *Tribunal supérieur de contentieux social* *Tribunal Superior de Asuntos de Seguridad Social*
Bundessozialgericht (BSG)	Federal Social Court *Cour fédérale de contentieux social* *Corte Federal de Asuntos de Seguridad Social*

Verwaltungsgericht (VerwG)	Administrative Court *Tribunal administratif* *Tribunal Contencioso-Administrativo*
Oberverwaltungsgericht/ *Verwaltungsgerichtshof* (OVerwG/VerwGH)	Higher Administrative Court *Tribunal administratif supérieur* *Tribunal Contencioso-Administrativo Superior*
Bundesverwaltungsgericht (BVerwG)	Federal Administrative Court *Cour fédérale administrative* *Corte Federal Contencioso-Administrativa*
Finanzgericht (FG)	Finance Court *Tribunal des Finances* *Tribunal de Hacienda*
Bundesfinanzhof (BFH)	Federal Finance Court *Cour fédérale des Finances* *Corte Federal de Hacienda*
Bundespatentgericht (BPG)	Federal Patents Court *Cour fédérale de Brevets* *Corte Federal de Patentes*
Bundesverfassungsgericht (BVG)	Federal Constitutional Court *Cour constitutionelle fédérale* *Corte Constitucional Federal*

6.5 The legal professions in Germany

Judges, prosecutors, lawyers and notaries all need a similar qualification, which they obtain after finishing their higher education degree and passing two very demanding official examinations (*Staatsexamen*). Between the first and second one, it is compulsory to spend a period of time acquiring practical experience in different areas (*Referendar*).

We have already commented on the role of the judges (Section 6.4). Let us add here that in Germany it is possible for university Law professors to be appointed as judges, as long as they comply with certain requisites established by law. The *Staatsanwalt* represents the state in criminal proceedings and is responsible for preliminary investigations, indictment and enforcement of convictions. In the BGH the prosecution may be pursued by the *Generalbundesanwalt* or by the *Bundesanwalt;* in the *OLG* by the *Generalstaatsanwalt* or by the *Staatsanwalt*; in the LG by the *Leitender Oberstaatsanwalt* or by the *Staatsanwalt*; and in the AG by the *Staatsanwalt* or by the *Amtsanwalt*. Being members of an administrative body, they are subject to hierarchical authority, but must always stay bound to the principle of legality.

The *Rechtsanwalt* represents and assists the parties inside and outside the courtroom by means of a power of attorney. As *Prozessbevollmächtigter* they are entitled to perform in all kinds of court, but some specific requisites apply in the case of the *Bundesgerichtshof.* Apart from strictly counseling, there are very many different areas of expertise in which they may use their professional skills, in the private as well as in the public sector. To mention just a few examples, they can be especially valuable candidates as mediators, consultants and advisors for banks, corporations and institutions, both private and public, or as board members in national and international organizations. Of course some of these positions may require additional specific qualifications, but in any case the possibilities are virtually endless. In some cases it is desirable and even necessary to have passed both official examinations, but on other occasions having passed the first one will suffice.

As for the *Notare*, on top of the general qualifications mentioned previously, they also require additional training as well as top marks in their second *Staatsexamen*. Even so, since restrictions apply for the effective number of notaries, there may be a need to wait for vacancies. Notaries can provide authoritative and independent legal advice and, in some *Länder*, they are also practicing lawyers. But above all, they have the capacity to authenticate legal transactions and testaments, and to certify the signatures on a document. Occasionally, notaries may be asked to keep goods or money in custody, especially in the event of contractual litigation.

Finally the *Rechtspfleger* act as auxiliary personnel. They belong to the higher echelon and are usually in charge of matters related to the voluntary jurisdiction. They also assist both the judge and the prosecutor in specific issues, including legal aid, writs of execution, the fixing of costs, enforcement of sentences, etc. They may be appointed to act as clerks of the court (*Urkundsbeamter der Geschäftsstelle*), responsible for a variety of tasks, which include extending certificates, maintaining records, extending copies of court documents, keeping minutes of the proceedings, keeping protocols and documents, etc.

PART III

The Common Law Tradition

As in the previous part centred on the civil law family, several legal systems belonging to the common law tradition are now analysed. To this aim, the focus is on the main aspects that are considered particularly useful for translators and interpreters in order to grasp the fundamentals of the different legal systems. Aspects related to particular branches of law, such as family law, contracts, criminal law, and the like are not discussed, given the large number of legal texts of various typologies and content that legal translators may encounter and the difficulty of deciding which ones would be most useful to concentrate on.

Even though the legal systems described and compared in the following chapters share a common language, the evolution of national law and the language itself has led to the fact that on occasions the same terms do not refer to the same realities in different countries. As an example, High Court in the United States refers to the US Supreme Court whereas in England it refers to a particular court that is not at the top of the jurisdictional system (see Section 7.4). It is for this reason that some of the exercises suggested in Chapter 11 are aimed at raising awareness about the dissimilarities in meaning that identical English terms can have in different legal systems.

CHAPTER 7

England and Wales

As discussed in Chapter 2, England and Wales have a different legal system to that of other territories of the British Isles. This section focuses on the analysis of the 'English' legal system understood as the one applying to both England and Wales.[1]

7.1 Historical evolution of the English legal system

The history of the English legal system has been already explained in Section 2.3, as it is the origin of the development of the common law system, which was later 'transplanted' to other parts of the world where this legal tradition was embraced.

7.2 Organization of law

The most salient features of the English legal system have also been described in Chapter 2.

---

1 The United Kingdom European Union referendum (known as the Brexit referendum) that took place on 23 June 2016 in the UK to get support for the continued membership on the EU resulted in a majority vote to leave the EU. If the UK effectively leaves the EU it will undoubtedly affect English law, one direct effect being that EU law will cease being a source of law in this country.

7.3 Sources of law in England and Wales

7.3.1 Legislation

Given the importance of case law in current English society and the fact
that England has a common law system in which judicial creativity plays a
fundamental role, legislation has become the main source of law nowadays.
Incidentally, England, unlike other common law countries, does not have
a written Constitution.

Parliament enjoys the power to enact legislation, or statutory laws, and
legislation can take the form of different instruments, the most important
of them being the Acts of Parliament (or primary legislation), which have
to be approved by the House of Commons and, with some exceptions, by
the House of Lords. Once approved, Acts of Parliament receive the Royal
Assent from the Queen.

Besides parliament, other bodies can also legislate under the authority
of primary legislation (under a specific power in the 'parent' or 'enabling'
Act), in what is known as secondary or delegated legislation. The legal
force and effect of delegated legislation is the same as that of the Act of
Parliament under which it has been enacted, to the extent that its enabling
Act authorizes it. There are various types of secondary legislation:

- Orders in Council: which permit the Government, through the Privy
  Council, to make law.
- Statutory instruments: regulations made by government ministers
  under powers delegated to them by parliament.
- Bylaws: made by local authorities, under the Local Government Act
  1972.

In addition, Court Rule Committees can issue rules governing procedures
in particular courts and some professions may also have some legislative
authority to regulate the conduct of their members.

The advantages of using delegated legislation are highlighted by authors
like Slapper and Kelly (2010: 46–7), who consider that it can be introduced

quickly and therefore saves time as 'rules can be changed in response to emergencies or unforeseen problems'. In addition, it is possible to have access to the particular expertise required to formulate this legislation, which is impossible when the legislation is enacted by parliament, where its members do not usually have that expertise. Finally, the use of secondary legislation allows for flexibility, as it is possible to respond to particular problems on an *ad hoc* basis.

As occurs in all member states in the European Union, EU law is a source of law in the United Kingdom.

7.3.2 Case law

Case law can be considered as the second source of law in England today. The doctrine of binding precedent is of utmost importance, given that England is a common law country, and is defined by Slapper and Kelly (*ibid.*: 49) as follows: 'within the hierarchical structure of the English courts, a decision of a higher court will be binding on a court lower than it in that hierarchy'. This doctrine means that when judges decide on cases, they have to verify whether a similar one has been previously decided upon by a higher court, in which case, the judge must follow the rule of law set in the earlier case. If a similar case has been previously decided by a lower court, the judge does not have to follow it but will have to take it into consideration. Case law is considered to have advantages as well as disadvantages. According to Slapper and Kelly (*ibid.*: 69–75), the following are the positives:

- Consistency: similar cases have to be decided on similar basis and decisions are not subject to the opinion of particular judges.
- Certainty: lawyers and clients can predict the outcome of a particular case.
- Efficiency: cases do not have to be reargued, what saves time to the judiciary, lawyers and clients.
- Flexibility: judges can develop law in certain areas without the parliament having to enact legislation.

However, case law is also criticized by Slapper and Kelly (*ibid.*: 75–7):

- Uncertainty: even if it we may think that it is possible to predict the outcome of a particular case, the vast number of cases that can be cited makes it difficult to be certain as to the results of a case. In addition, judges can select which case to follow through the mechanism of distinguishing cases by the facts.
- Fixity: the law may become ossified due to an unfair precedent and therefore injustices can perpetuate.
- Unconstitutionality: this calls to question the role of the judiciary, whether they should be making law or simply applying it.

7.3.3 Custom

Some specific local customs still operate today as a secondary source of law in England and Wales and the parties involved may affirm the existence of customary practices in order to support their case. To be recognized, Slapper and Kelly (*ibid.*: 80) state that a custom must satisfy the following requirements:

- have existed from 'time immemorial', that is, since 1189;
- have been exercised continuously within that period, peacefully and without opposition;
- have been felt to be obligatory and consistent with other customs;
- be able to be define with precision;
- be reasonable.

7.4 The English court system

The courts of England are integrated into the HM Courts and Tribunals Service, which was created on 1 April 2011 to provide support for the administration of justice in courts and tribunals. As an agency of the Ministry of Justice, it is responsible for the administration of the criminal, civil and family courts and tribunals in England and Wales as well as the non-devolved tribunals in Scotland and Northern Ireland. It provides for a fair, efficient and effective justice system delivered by an independent judiciary. According to the description given by the Ministry of Justice (<www.just ice.gov.uk/about/hmcts>), the HM Courts and Tribunals Service aims to ensure that all citizens receive timely access to justice on the base of their different needs, whether as victims or witnesses of crime, defendants accused of crimes, consumers in debt, children at risk of harm, businesses involved in commercial disputes or individuals asserting their employment rights or challenging the decisions of government bodies.

Courts in England can be broadly divided into two main groups: civil courts and criminal courts. The former deal with civil cases involving individuals or corporate bodies, while the latter look after cases brought by the state against individual or corporate defendants. A tribunal, not to be confused with a court, is a body outside the court structure, where disputes relating to areas such as immigration, employment and some tax matters are heard and adjudicate on. Tribunals are thought to be a cheap and fast way to allow expert knowledge to be applied (<http://webarchive. nationalarchives.gov.uk/20130128112038/> and <http://www.justice.gov. uk/courts/glossary-of-terms/glossary-of-terms-legal#t>).

In the next few pages, the civil and criminal courts of England are discussed according to information extracted from sources such as the website Justice (<www.justice.gov.uk>) and the works by Zweigert and Kötz (1998), De Cruz (2007), and Slapper and Kelly (2010).

The figure below visually illustrates the court system in England and Wales (see Figure 6).

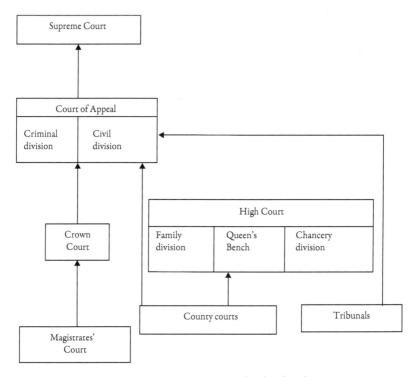

Figure 6: Court system in England and Wales.

7.4.1 Magistrates' courts

Magistrates' courts deal both with criminal and private law. As they are responsible for the resolution of 97 per cent of criminal cases, they can be considered a key part of the criminal justice system. They mainly deal with traffic offences and their procedure is without a jury. When it comes to private law, they administer cases on anti-social behaviour or public health and are responsible for the enforcement of fines and community sentences. They also deal with family proceedings such as adoption, maintenance to spouses and children, and applications for residence and contact orders. In situations of domestic violence, they issue personal protection orders and exclusion orders. Cases that involve a penalty above the magistrates' sentencing powers or that tackle more serious crimes requiring the presence of a jury are sent to the Crown Court.

7.4.2 County courts

The county courts adjudicate on small-scale litigation and that is why they are often referred to as the small claims court. They deal with civil or private law matters, among which: claims for debt repayment, including enforcing court orders and return of goods bought on credit; personal injury; breach of contract concerning goods or property; family issues such as relationship breakdowns or adoption; and housing disputes, including mortgage and council rent arrears as well as re-possession. These courts are of great practical importance since most civil actions are heard in them.

7.4.3 The Crown Court

Together with the High Court of Justice and the Court of Appeal, the Crown Court is one of the Senior Courts of England. It is not a local court but a single one, which sits in over ninety centres in England and Wales, and deals with serious criminal offences such as murder, rape or robbery, some of which are on appeal or have been referred from magistrates' courts. Trials are heard by a judge and a jury made up of twelve individuals. Members of the public are selected for jury service or may be required to go to court as witnesses.

7.4.4 The High Court

The High Court deals with civil disputes within three administrative divisions:

- The Queen's Bench Division: the main common law court, with criminal and appellate jurisdiction, it deals mainly with claims for damage in respect of personal injury, negligence, breach of contract, libel and slander (defamation), non-payment of a debt, and possession of land or property. In certain cases, for instance claims to do with negligence by solicitors or with possession of land, the claimant has a choice as to whether to bring the claim in the Queen's Bench Division or in the Chancery Division. The Queen's Bench Division includes the Divisional Court, the Admiralty Court, the Commercial Court and the Technology and Construction Court. Its workings, with certain exceptions, are governed by the Civil Procedure Rules (CPR).

- The Chancery Division: deals mainly with business and property related disputes, competition, patents claims, intellectual property claims, insolvency claims, trust claims, probate claims and resolves questions of company law. It also hears appeals to the High Court. Like the Queen's Bench Division, it contains several specialist courts: the Patents Court and the Bankruptcy and Companies Court.
- The Family Division: has jurisdiction to deal with all matrimonial matters, the Children Act 1989 and the Child Abduction and Custody Act 1985. It also takes care of matters relating to Part IV Family Law Act 1996 (Family Homes and Domestic Violence), Adoption Section Inheritance Act 1975 applications, and Probate and Court of Protection work.

7.4.5 The Court of Appeal

The Court of Appeal consists of the civil and criminal divisions. The latter hears appeals from the Crown Court, whereas the Civil Division hears them from:

- The three divisions of the High Court, i.e. Chancery, Queen's Bench and Family Division.
- The county courts across England and Wales.
- Certain tribunals such as the Employment Appeal Tribunal, the Immigration Appeal Tribunal, the Lands Tribunal and the Social Security Commissioners.

The Court of Appeal, the highest one within the above-mentioned Senior Courts, usually requires the presence of three judges to hear an appeal. However, five may sit for very important cases and some cases may be heard by two judges only, for reasons of efficiency. Although the Court is presided by the Lord Chancellor, in practice this role is performed by the 'Master of the Rolls'.

7.4.6 The Supreme Court

The Supreme Court is the final court of appeal in the UK for civil cases, and for criminal cases in England, Wales and Northern Ireland. Judicial authority was transferred from the House of Lords to the Supreme Court on 1 October 2009, thus creating a single jurisdiction on appeal in the UK, including Scotland, for civil cases. As well as being the final court of appeal, it plays an important role in the development of UK law. As an appeal court, it cannot consider a case unless a relevant order has been made in a lower court. It hears appeals on arguable points of law of general public importance, concentrates on cases of the greatest public and constitutional importance and maintains and develops the role of the highest court in the UK as a leader in the common law world. In England and Wales, the Supreme Court hears appeals from the Court of Appeal (Civil Division), the Court of Appeal (Criminal Division) and, on special occasions, the High Court.

7.4.7 Tribunals

Tribunals are specialist judicial bodies which decide disputes in particular areas of law. Appeals to tribunals are generally against a decision made by a Government department or agency, with the exception of the Employment Tribunal where cases are on a party versus party basis (i.e. employee versus employer). There are tribunals in England, Wales, Scotland and Northern Ireland covering a wide range of areas affecting day-to-day life. Appeals to the First-tier Tribunal are against the decisions from government departments and other public bodies. The Upper Tribunal hears appeals from the First-tier Tribunal on points of law, such as the interpretation of a legal principle or statute. Further appeals may be made, with permission, to the Court of Appeal. Tribunals often sit as a panel comprising a judge, who is legally qualified, and other non-legal members such as doctors, chartered surveyors, ex-service personnel and accountants. However, in some jurisdictions cases may be heard by a judge or member sitting alone. Tribunals adopt procedures that are less complicated and more informal than those typically associated with the courts.

7.5 The legal professions in England

As with the legal systems analysed so far, the focus is now on the members of the legal professions in England: the judiciary, solicitors, barristers, legal executives and clerks to the Justices.

7.5.1 The judiciary

Judges in England interpret and apply the law and, on occasions, they even create it. Their role is of utmost importance in determining the scope and the interpretation of the law, given the importance of case law in this country. There are different types of judges sitting in courts or tribunals, each hearing different cases and with different powers to use when deciding the outcomes. They sit in the three main jurisdictions: civil, criminal and family.

Judges at magistrates' courts are called Justices of the Peace and do not need any legal training. They are unpaid members of their local community, work part-time and deal with the less serious criminal cases, such as minor theft, criminal damage, public disorder and motoring offences. Exceptions to this rule can be found in larger towns, where magistrates with legal training can be found (Zweigert and Kötz, 1998: 206). In addition, a smaller number of district judges, full-time members of the judiciary who hear cases in magistrates' courts, can be found. They usually deal with the longer and more complex matters coming before these courts.

At the county courts there are district judges, who deal with the majority of cases, and circuit judges. They are appointed to one of seven regions of England and Wales, and sit in the Crown and county courts within their particular region. It is also possible to find different categories of the judiciary at the High Court:

- High Court judges, assigned to one of the three divisions of the High Court, namely, the Chancery Division, the Queen's Bench and the Family Division.
- Chancellor of the High Court, the head of the Chancery Division.
- President of the Queen's Bench Division, responsible for the work in the Queen's Bench Division.
- President of the Family Division, who heads this division of the High Court.
- Masters and registrars, who are procedural judges for the majority of civil matters in the Chancery and Queen's Bench Divisions.

The judges of the Court of Appeal are the Heads of Division and the Lords Justices of Appeal, of whom the leading judge, or Head of Division, in charge of the civil cases is the Master of the Rolls, or Head of Civil Justice. This professional presides over the most difficult and sensitive cases. The Lord Chief Justice became head of the judiciary of England and Wales in 2006, a role previously held by the Lord Chancellor. Tribunal judges are legally qualified people who render the tribunals' decisions, sometimes alone and sometimes with the assistance of other panel members, who may not be legally qualified but participate in the process based on their expertise.

7.5.2 *Solicitors*

Solicitors and barristers are the two professions authorized to provide legal services in England and Wales. The former are lawyers who deal directly with clients and who engage the services of a counsel (barrister) when litigation is required. Solicitors usually assist the client in the initial stages of the case and have the monopoly of certain practices (for instance, they are the only ones authorized to give final endorsement in conveyancing). Solicitors have recently lost their monopoly in certain areas but gained the right to perform other tasks, such as litigation, granted by the Courts and Legal Services Act 1990 and Access to Justice Act 1999, according to which solicitors, and no longer only barristers, have the right of audience before every court (Slapper and Kelly 2010).

Solicitors have a governing body, the Law Society, which has been overseen by the independent regulatory body, the Solicitors Regulation Authority, since 2007. The job of this authority is to regulate and discipline all solicitors in England and Wales and its main aim is to generate confidence in the profession among the public (*ibid.*).

7.5.3 *Barristers*

Barristers are, in essence, court advocates although they also perform other functions such as drafting statements of cases and writing advices for solicitors (*ibid.*: 330). Normally, they do not deal directly with clients and they have to be engaged by a solicitor. Until recently (Courts and Legal Services Act 1990 and Access to Justice Act 1999), they had the monopoly of advocacy before the courts, now shared with solicitors.

Barristers associate at the Bar, an association of the members of the Inns of Court in London, which is the professional association for barristers in England and Wales. Today, there are four Inns of Court: Inner Temple, Middle Temple, Lincoln's Inn and Gray's Inn. Barristers are *junior counsels* until they 'take silk' and become Queen's Counsel, i.e. senior barristers of special merit (*ibid.*). They work in offices called 'chambers', most of them run by barristers' clerks who act as business managers, allocating work to the various barristers and negotiating their fees.

7.5.4 Other legal professions

Other legal professions include the legal executives and the clerks to the Justices. The former are members of a regulated profession, normally self-employed or employed by a solicitor, and they provide legal services for solicitors and conduct unregulated legal work for public businesses. They belong to the Chartered Institute of Legal Executives (CILEX). The clerks to the Justices provide legal advice to the Justices of the Peace at the magistrates' courts.

CHAPTER 8

The United States

Although the United States originally received the common law of England, their legal organization has evolved in such a way that it is nowadays very different from that in England. As Atiyah and Summers (1991: 417) point out, 'these two legal systems embrace very different conceptions of law'. The law of the US comprises Federal and State laws, as well as constitutional law. In addition, the vastness and complexity of the territory, the variegated foreign influences, the coexistence of different legal systems (that of Louisiana belongs to the Civil tradition), and the changes undergone in the development of legal concepts and principles have shaped a unique and distinctive legal system (De Cruz 2007: 108).

8.1 Historical evolution of the US legal system

The US legal system can be symbolically dated to 1607, when the first English settlement took place in Jamestown, Virginia. From that date, legislation started to progress in the 13 colonies, although it developed at a different pace and in different stages depending on when each colony was established and when they issued their charters. English settlers brought with them the law with which they were familiar, not necessarily the common law administered by the courts of Westminster, but also local customs, as they existed in their villages and boroughs. When society became more complex, shipping, commerce and industry expanded and so did common law. Colonial courts were established, although not ecclesiastical courts, and appeals were directed to London. Trials by jury, both in civil and criminal cases, were adopted.

In 1774 the First Continental Congress took place in Philadelphia, with approximately fifty-five delegates from all the colonies, thus showing one of the first signs of unity between the colonies and of disquiet against England. There was, however, a feeling that the individual rights of the English and the Bill of Rights of 1689 should be followed and introduced in the colonies (De Cruz 2007). When independence arrived in 1776, the colonies had developed a legal profession with considerable social standing, English common law had already become the basis of the legal systems of the 13 colonies, and it was highly regarded and considered essential to the growing commercial needs. However, different dates as to when English law would cease to apply were established and some colonies reacted against the application of English law and prohibited the citation of English decisions rendered after independence. As a break with England, written constitutions began to appear in the different states and in 1787 the Federal constitution was adopted. Louisiana, purchased from the French in 1803 and admitted to the Federation in 1812, continued to follow the civil law tradition and adopted several codifications based on the French model, including the civil code (*ibid.*).

The anti-British feeling, together with the fact that there was no body of American case law to replace the English decisions, made French and Roman law ideal candidates to replace the gap in the law. Nonetheless, civil law failed to find its way in the US, mainly due to the fact that most judges were not proficient in foreign languages. Therefore, English law continued to be applied, as a simplified version of the law in England, so long as it did not contradict the constitutional, political or geographical conditions of the new states. It was not until the beginning of the nineteenth century that the scholarly writing tradition began and the American law school was established, coinciding with a revived interest in the English tradition. The foundations for contracts, torts, sale of goods, real property and conflict of laws were laid during this period, although local customs and usages were also adopted. Codification also reached the United States and, following the model of the French code, some states adopted codes, such as Massachusetts and New York (*ibid.*).

8.2 Organization of law

The US is a Federal state to which the Constitution explicitly grants specific powers. All powers not expressly delegated to the Federal state remain within the states, which have their own constitution, governmental structure, legal courts and judiciary. Federal law is supreme only in limited areas and separation of powers exists: legislative, judicial and executive.

Laws have been created on the basis of English common law, and the same institutional and conceptual frameworks are applied to the judiciary, who follow the same approach and basically the same procedure, albeit a simplified version. However, as previously mentioned, laws are usually classified into codes, in accordance with the civil law tradition. But this codification does not follow a plan; it is more a pragmatic and empirical case–oriented approach which does not lend itself to generalizations (Farnsworth 1987). In spite of this, three broad divisions in US law must be taken into account.

8.2.1 Law and equity

The existing system of equity, inherited from England, was integrated into the law. In some states there were even separate courts for law and equity and others had a single system in which a court could sit as a law court or as an equity court, depending on the case (*ibid.*). By the middle of the nineteenth century there was a demand for the merger of the two systems, a process that began in 1848 with the adoption of the Field Code in New York. The two systems were finally merged by the Federal courts in 1938, in practically all the states, although today there are still some states which administer law and equity separately: Alabama, Arkansas, Delaware, Mississippi and Tennessee (De Cruz 2007).

8.2.2 *Substantive law and procedural law*

This difference is also found in legal systems belonging to other legal traditions (see Chapter 2) and it refers to the positive law applied (substantive law) and, as explained by Farnsworth (1987: 85), to:

> all the aspects of the conduct of legal controversy before the courts, including access to the courts, who may sue and be sued, the form of the action, the availability of countervailing claims, the conditions of maintaining suit, the steps before trial, the method of proof, the effects of the court's judgements, remedies, and appeals (procedural or adjective law).

Procedural or adjective law includes both civil and criminal procedures and the law of evidence. This distinction is particularly important in the US because, as Farnsworth (*ibid.*) underlines, 'if a statute concerns a matter of "procedure" rather than "substance", it will be unaffected by constitutional prohibitions against retroactive legislation'.

8.2.3 *Public law and private law*

Even if the court system in the US is not divided into public and private law courts, it is possible to differentiate between matters of public law and those which fall under the sphere of private law. Similarly to what happens in other countries, particularly in civil law countries where the distinction between public and private law is of utmost importance, matters included in public law are mainly administrative, constitutional or from criminal law, whilst private law covers family law, contracts, torts, property law or commercial law.

8.3 Sources of law in the US

8.3.1 Primary legislation

The US Constitution is the supreme law of the United States to which all other legislative sources are subject and it establishes the boundaries of federal law. Under the hierarchy of the Constitution, there are several levels of federal law. However, contrary to what could be expected, federal law is supreme only in limited areas (De Cruz 2007). International treaties signed by the US, after ratification by the Senate, have equal authority with federal statutes and are subject to the Constitution. In cases of conflict between a treaty and a federal statute, the last one to have been adopted prevails (Farnsworth 1987). The Constitution gives Congress the authority to enact laws, which are subject only to the Constitution and are at the same hierarchical level as the international treaties signed by the US President.

At a lower level are federal executive orders and administrative rules and regulations. As Farnsworth (*ibid.*) points out, these can be enacted by the President, who has limited power to issue executive orders and these tend to be usually legislative in character. Federal administrative bodies may also have the power to make rules and regulations of legislative character.

As far as state legislation is concerned, all states have their own constitution, which is the main legal source in the state itself though still subject to federal legislation. States also have the power to enact legislation, so long as it does not contradict federal legislation or the state constitution. In fact, 'state statutes are, for the common lawyer, the most common form of legislation' (*ibid.*: 57). As with federal bodies, state administrative bodies may also enact administrative rules and regulations to take care of certain activities within the state. Finally, local administrative units, which vary depending on the particular state, may also have legislative powers to issue municipal charters, ordinances, rules and regulations.

As a common law country, the US follows the doctrine of precedent in case law. However, the role of the judge as a law creator is secondary in the United States nowadays. Towards the end of the nineteenth century, judges ceased being law creators to become administrators and interpreters of the law, since the system of judicial decisions on a case-by-case basis could not respond to rapid political, economic and social change. Legislation was thus seen as an instrument of change, consolidation and adaptation and was used to cope with the needs of a new society (De Cruz 2007).

8.3.2 Secondary legislation

Secondary legislation in the US includes treatises, legal periodicals, encyclopaedias and aids to finding and interpreting primary legislation. Its value is persuasive, as judges are not bound to follow it, contrary to what happens with statutes or cases. In practice, however, judges frequently cite secondary legislation in their opinions (Farnsworth 1987).

8.4 The United States court system

The Constitution establishes the judicial branch of the federal government and specifies the authority of the federal courts, which have exclusive jurisdiction only over certain types of cases, such as those involving federal laws, foreign governments, or controversies between US states. In certain other areas, federal courts share jurisdiction with state courts, i.e. both federal and state courts may decide cases involving parties who live in different states. State courts have exclusive jurisdiction over the vast majority of cases.

Parties have a right to trial by jury in all criminal and most civil cases. A jury usually consists of a panel of six to twenty-three citizens, depending on the case and the type of jury, who hear the evidence and apply the law stated by the judge to reach a decision based on the facts. More specifically, the Petit or Trial Jury (six to twelve people) fairly and impartially decides the facts in a trial in criminal cases whilst in civil cases its role is to decide whether the defendant injured the plaintiff. The Grand Jury (sixteen to twenty-three people) acts only in criminal cases and decides if there is enough evidence against a defendant to file an indictment charging him or her with a crime. However, most legal disputes in the US are resolved before the case reaches a jury, by legal motion or settlement, and not by trial (Federal Judicial Center n.d.).

8.4.1 Federal system of courts

The US Constitution establishes the US Supreme Court and gives Congress the authority to establish the lower federal courts. Congress has established two levels of federal courts below the Supreme Court: US District Courts and US Circuit Courts of Appeals (see Figure 7):

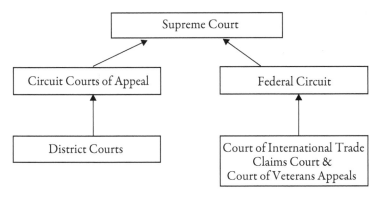

Figure 7: The United States court system.

District Courts, the courts of first instance in the federal system, amount to ninety-four, organized into twelve regional circuits distributed throughout the nation and at least one of them is located in each state. In addition to district judges (who sit individually to hear cases), bankruptcy judges (who hear only bankruptcy cases) and magistrate judges (who perform many judicial duties under the general supervision of district judges) are located within the District Courts.

Circuit Courts of Appeals can be found on the next level. Panels of three judges hear appeals from the District Courts. A party to a case may appeal as a matter of right to the Circuit Court of Appeals, and the government has no right of appeal in a criminal case if the verdict is 'not guilty'. Regional Circuit Courts also hear appeals from decisions of federal administrative agencies. One non-regional circuit court, the Federal Circuit, hears appeals in specialized cases involving patent laws and claims against the federal government.

At the top of the federal court system is the US Supreme Court, made up of nine justices who sit together to hear cases. At its discretion, the Supreme Court may hear appeals from the Federal Circuit Courts of Appeals as well as from the highest state courts if the appeal involves the US Constitution or federal law.

8.4.2   US court system

Although the structure of state court systems varies from state to state, each one with unique features, some generalizations can be made. Most states have courts of limited jurisdiction presided over by a single judge who hears minor civil and criminal cases. States also have general jurisdiction trial courts that are presided over by a single judge. These trial courts are usually called Circuit courts or Superior courts and hear major civil and criminal cases. Some states have specialized courts that hear only certain cases related to traffic or family law. All states have a highest court, usually called State Supreme Court, which serves as an appellate court. Many states also have an intermediate appellate court, called Court of appeals, which hears appeals from the trial court. A party in a case generally has one right of appeal.

8.5   The legal professions in the US

The main legal professions in the United States are judges, prosecutors and lawyers.

8.5.1 Judges

Justices of the US Supreme Court and circuit and district judges are appointed by the President of the United States if approved by a majority vote of the US Senate. They serve 'during good behaviour', usually a life term, and tend to be distinguished lawyers, Law professors, or judges from lower federal or state courts. Federal judges may only be removed from office through an impeachment process in which charges are made by the House of Representatives and a trial is conducted by the Senate. These protective mechanisms allow federal judges to exercise independent judgment without political or outside interference or influence, in accordance with the principle of separation of powers. The methods of selecting state judges vary from state to state and are often different within a state, depending on the type of court. The most common selection systems are by commission nomination and by popular election. In the commission nomination system, judges are appointed by the governor, i.e. the state's chief executive, who must choose from a list of candidates selected by an independent commission made up of lawyers, legislators, lay citizens, and sometimes judges. In many states, judges are selected by popular election. Candidates must meet certain qualifications, such as being a practising lawyer for a certain number of years. With very few exceptions, state judges serve specified, renewable terms.

There is no specific course of training for judges and no examination. Some states require judges to attend initial and continuing education programmes to learn about developments in the law, usually offered within the federal and state court systems. Atiyah and Summers (1991) highlight some interesting divergences amongst English and American judges based on their different academic backgrounds, training, selection process, pay scales or the fact that English judges tend to show a more pragmatic attitude versus the more political bias of American judges.

8.5.2 Prosecutors

Prosecutors in the federal system are part of the executive branch of the Department of Justice. The Attorney General of the US, who heads the Department of Justice, is appointed by the President with Senate confirmation. The chief prosecutors in the federal court districts are called US attorneys and are also appointed by the President with Senate confirmation. States also have an Attorney General in the state executive branch, who is usually elected by the citizens of that state. There are also prosecutors in different regions of the state, called state's attorneys or district attorneys, who are also usually elected.

According to Standard 3–1.2(c) of the Criminal Justice Standards, the duty of the prosecutor is to seek justice, not merely to convict. In addition, paragraph (d) of the same Standard 3–1.2 stresses that it 'is an important function of the prosecutor to seek to reform and improve the administration of criminal justice. When inadequacies or injustices in the substantive or procedural law come to prosecutor's attention, he or she should stimulate efforts for remedial action'.

8.5.3 Lawyers

Lawyers in the US legal system are also known as attorneys, attorneys-at-law, counsellors or counsellors-at-law. They are the professionals legally qualified to prosecute and defend actions in court. A difference found with regard to other legal systems is that there is no formal distinction among types of legal practice, that is, the US legal system does not differentiate between lawyers who plead in court and those who do not, as it is the case in England, for instance, where solicitors coexist with barristers (see Section 7.5).

Having its roots in the common law tradition, the US legal system uses the adversarial process, in which lawyers are essential to the process as they are responsible for presenting their clients' evidence and legal arguments to the court. Based on the lawyers' statements, a judge or jury determines the facts and applies the law to reach a decision before judgment is entered.

Individuals are free to represent themselves in US courts, but lawyers are often necessary to present cases effectively. There is no national authority that warrants lawyers and these are licensed by the individual states in which they practise law. Most states require applicants to hold a law degree (Juris Doctor) from an accredited law school. A law degree in the US is a post-graduate degree awarded at the end of a three-year course of study, though most individuals complete four years of college/university before attending law school. Many states require that applicants for a license to practise law pass a written bar examination and meet certain standards of character. Some states may allow lawyers to become bar members based on membership in another state's bar. All states provide for out-of-state lawyers to practise in the state in a particular case under certain conditions. Lawyers can engage in any kind of practice.

CHAPTER 9

Ireland

Reference to Ireland in this chapter is to the Republic of Ireland, as Northern Ireland is part of the United Kingdom of Great Britain and Northern Ireland, where three different legal systems coexist (see Chapter 2).

9.1 Historical evolution of the Irish legal system

Ireland was the first recipient of the English system of law, which, prior to the sixteenth century, was only enforced in the Pale, a territory around Dublin. Outside this area, native customs and rules, known as Brehon law, were applied even if they were declared by the English kings as contrary to English law and, subsequently, of no effect. Brehon law was administered by Brehons, the successors to Celtic druids, and whilst similar to judges, their role was closer to that of an arbitrator. Their task was to preserve and interpret the law rather than to expand it. The end of Brehon law's authority was signalled by the Proclamation of King James I in 1603, which received the Irish people into the King's protection. The country was subsequently divided into counties and English law was administered throughout the country. From then on, English rule was a practical reality in Ireland and all laws passed in England until 1800 had effect in Ireland, and some of them even continue to have effect now. Also, the court system established in Ireland during the nineteenth century was created mirroring the system which had existed in England since the Norman Conquest in 1066. In 1800 the Act of Union was signed, dissolving the Irish parliament and establishing the Westminster Parliament in London as the sole legislative body of the United Kingdom of Great Britain and Ireland. The Act centralized all government power in London until 1922, when the Anglo-Irish Treaty of 1921, signed by representatives of the Provisional Irish government and the British government, came into force and established the Irish Free State or *Saorstát Éireann* (Byrne and McCutcheon 1990, 2009).

The country had been partitioned in 1920 when, in an effort to resolve the Irish question, Westminster passed the Government of Ireland Act, and divided Ireland into Northern Ireland and Southern Ireland, each with its own parliament. Both parliaments would be ultimately subject to the English parliament and would be required to send some members to sit in Westminster. The Constitution for the Free State was approved in 1922, although the lack of agreement about whether the Anglo-Irish Treaty should have been signed caused a split in the country and a new Constitution was drafted and put to Referendum to the People of Ireland in 1937.

9.2 Organization of law

As discussed above, the Irish legal system belongs to the common law tradition and as such it shares the main features of this family. However, due to the country's unique historical and social development, there are some characteristics that differentiate it from its parent legal system, especially the existence of a Constitution to which all legislation must comply (in the manner of the US Constitution) and the fact that case law does not occupy a pre-eminent position as a source of law, whilst legislation holds a privileged place.

In addition, Irish law has traditionally differentiated between substantive law and procedural or adjective law. The former includes the type of legal subjects that allow for rights and obligations and liabilities, whilst the latter implements the former and encompasses civil and criminal procedure as well as the law of evidence. Irish substantive law differentiates between public and private law, in the same manner as in other legal systems belonging to the civil law tradition and as it has been already described in the case of the United States (see Chapter 8).

9.3 Sources of law in Ireland

The primary source of law in Ireland is the 1937 Constitution, *Bunreacht na h'Éireann*, which designates the National Parliament, the *Oireachtas*, as the sole law-making institution in the state. Legislation is the second source of law and includes not only laws passed by the *Oireachtas* but also by those parliaments with jurisdiction over Ireland before 1922. As Ireland is a member state of the European Union, EU legislation is also a source of law. The common law rules that were developed prior to independence continued to be applied and where legislation has not yet been passed to deal with a particular area of law, the judges – case law – continue to be the only source of law to be applied in such situations. Case law constitutes the third source of law.

In addition, there are also secondary sources of law, as is the case in other legal systems: law textbooks, legal journals and legal scholars' work that have helped to develop the law.

9.3.1 *The 1937 Constitution,* Bunreacht na h'Éireann

As explained by Byrne and McCutcheon (1990), the 1937 Constitution was designed as a way to break free from former connections with British rule, represented by the remnants of the Anglo-Irish Treaty of 1921. It is the basic law of the State and provides for its basic structure, divided into the classical three branches of government: the executive or cabinet (headed by the President or *An Taoiseach*), the legislative power (National Parliament or *Oireachtas*) and the judicial branch.

9.3.2 Legislation

Laws passed by the parliament are the second source of law in Ireland. The parliament, or *Oireachtas*, consists of the President of Ireland and two Houses: the House of Representatives or *Dáil Éireann* and the Senate, called *Seanad Éireann*. The President of Ireland is the Head of State and commander-in-chief of the armed forces, but does not have the executive powers assigned, for example, to the President of the United States.

The *Oireachtas* is the sole body making legislation in Ireland today. Legislation cannot be contrary to the Constitution or it would be invalid. Laws passed before the enactment of the 1937 Constitution have full force as long as they are not inconsistent with the Constitution. It is interesting to note, for terminological reasons, that when legislation is proceeding through the *Oireachtas* it is known as a Bill and once it has been signed by the President, it becomes an Act of the *Oireachtas*. Acts of the Parliament are usually referred to as primary legislation but there is also secondary (or delegated) legislation. The Acts of the *Oireachtas* state that, 'in order to implement the basic principles contained in the Act, more detailed laws may be required' (Byrne and McCutcheon *ibid.*: 19). These laws usually take the form of regulations or orders and are made by the minister in charge of that particular area. Finally, we cannot forget the role of EU legislation in Ireland, as in the other European countries belonging to the European Union. For a classification of EU law, please refer to Chapter 3.

9.3.3 Case law

Being a common law system, a large number of rules have developed originally from judges. Even if the parliament has the exclusive power of passing legislation, the judges have an important role in applying the law and interpreting it, thus they pay great attention to previous decisions made in similar cases in the past. The laws that were applied in Ireland before 1922 emanated from the English system and were maintained after independence. In some areas, this is still the case and Irish lawyers and judges still continue to refer to decisions from the English courts even if, as discussed by Byrne and McCutcheon (*ibid.*), these are now decisions from foreign courts. The most important judgements in Ireland are published on a regular basis in book form, known as the law reports.

9.3.4 Secondary sources of law

Textbooks and periodicals, although not sources of law, may have an important effect on Irish law development, the same as intellectual influences and legal scholars' work. The main influence, as cited by Byrne and McCutcheon (*ibid.*), derives from the close links with England until 1922, as during the mid-nineteenth century England was one of the great world powers. The second main influence stems from the 1937 Constitution, with its foundations on the theological philosophy behind Judaeo-Christian teaching (*ibid.*), the concept of natural law, or the idea of protection of fundamental human rights.

9.4 The Irish court system

The court system in Ireland has its origins in the 1922 Constitution, which promoted the creation of new courts to replace those that had evolved under the British administration. The Courts of Justice Act 1924 set out the legal basis for a court system and was the trigger for the establishment of the new courts. According to the Irish Courts Service (<www.courts.ie>), the current courts were established by the Courts (Establishment and Constitution) Act 1961 pursuant to Article 34 of the 1937 Constitution. Articles 34 to 37 of the Constitution deal with the administration of justice in general and article 34.1 states that 'Justice shall be administered in Courts established by law'.

The Constitution outlines the structure of the court system (see Figure 8) as comprising a court of final appeal, the Supreme Court, and various courts of first instance, including a High Court with full jurisdiction in all criminal and civil matters and courts of limited jurisdiction such as the Circuit Court and the District Court, both organized on a regional basis.

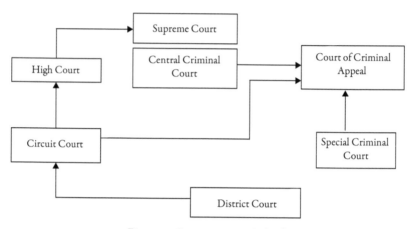

Figure 8: Court system in Ireland.

The Supreme Court is the court of final appeal, though it also has original jurisdiction. Its main task is to hear appeals from decisions of the High Court and it can also deal with matters referred to it by the Circuit Court, when a question of law arises and the parties seek an opinion. It can also hear appeals from the Court of Criminal Appeal, but only when the latter itself, the Attorney General or the Director of Public Prosecutions certify that the decision involves a point of law of exceptional public importance and that it is desirable, in the public interest, that an appeal should be taken to the Supreme Court on that point of law. The original jurisdiction allows the Supreme Court to decide on the constitutionality of a bill if it is referred to it by the President and can also determine on the permanent incapacity of the President, if it arises.

The High Court has original full jurisdiction and power to determine all matters, civil or criminal, whether of law or fact. It can also determine the validity of any law with regard to the Constitution. It hears appeals from the Circuit Court in civil matters and has the authority to review the decisions of certain tribunals. It may also give rulings on questions of law submitted by the District Court. In criminal matters, a person granted bail in the District Court may apply to the High Court to vary the conditions of bail. If the District Court refuses bail, an application may be made to the High Court. A person charged with murder can only apply to the High Court for bail. When exercising its criminal jurisdiction, the High Court is known as the Central Criminal Court.

The Circuit Court is a court of limited and local jurisdiction organized on a regional basis. The work of this court can be divided into four main areas: civil, criminal, family law and jury service. The Circuit Court sits in venues in each circuit. Sittings vary in length from one day to three weeks and are generally held every two to four months in each venue in the circuit. Dublin and Cork have continual sittings throughout each legal term. In civil matters, it hears claims up to the value of €75,000. For family law, it is competent for matters of divorce, judicial separation, nullity and other ancillary matters. In criminal matters, the Circuit Court has the same jurisdiction as the Central Criminal Court in all indictable offences except murder, rape, aggravated sexual assault, treason, piracy and related offences. The Circuit Criminal Court is responsible for jury selection and this responsibility rests with the County Registrar in each of the twenty-six counties. It hears appeals from the District Court in all matters and it also acts as an appeal court for appeals from the decisions of the Labour Court, Unfair Dismissals Tribunal and the Employment Appeals Tribunal.

Ireland is divided into twenty-three districts, with one or more judges permanently assigned to each District Court, plus one Dublin Metropolitan District. District Courts judge cases on civil, criminal, family law and licensing business, the wider jurisdiction being in the family law area (domestic violence, guardianship of children, maintenance or child care).

The Court of Criminal Appeal deals with appeals by persons convicted on indictment in the Circuit Court, Special Criminal Court or Central Criminal Court, the latter being the criminal division of the High Court. It tries serious crimes, including murder, rape, treason and piracy. The Special Criminal Court was established to hear and try offences in those cases where it is determined that the ordinary courts are inadequate to secure the effective administration of justice and for the preservation of public peace and order.

As for trials with minors, there is a special court in the cities of Cork, Limerick and Waterford, called the Children Court, where charges against children under sixteen years of age are heard. The judge has the prerogative to reject charges due to their gravity or other special circumstances. For any offence, except homicide, the District Court has jurisdiction to try a child or a young person provided that, in the case of an indictable offence, the child's parent or the young person has been informed of their right to trial by jury and has consented to be dealt with summarily.

9.5 The legal professions in Ireland

The next sections focus on the following professionals who take part in the legal process in Ireland: the judiciary, solicitors and barristers.

9.5.1 The judiciary

Following the principle of separation of powers, judges are completely independent in the performance of their functions and are appointed by the President of Ireland under Article 35.1 of the Constitution, on the advice of the Government. Those appointed must make the Declaration provided for in Article 34.5.1 of the Constitution of Ireland not later than ten days after the date of appointment. According to the Association of Judges of Ireland (<www.aji.ie>), precedence and rank within the judiciary is as follows:

1. The Chief Justice.
2. The President of the High Court (ex-officio a judge of the Supreme Court).
3. The judges of the Supreme Court who are former Chief Justices each according to priority of his or her appointment as Chief Justice.

4. Other judges of the Supreme Court, other than judges of the High Court who (being former Presidents of the High Court) are ex-officio judges of the Supreme Court, each according to priority of his or her appointment as an ordinary judge of the Supreme Court.
5. Judges of the High Court who (being former Presidents of the High Court) are ex-officio judges of the Supreme Court, each according to priority of his or her appointment as President of the High Court.
6. Other judges of the High Court, other than judges of the Circuit Court who (being a President or a former President of the Circuit Court) are ex-officio judges of the High Court, each according to priority of his or her appointment as an ordinary judge of the High Court.
7. The President of the Circuit Court (ex officio a judge of the High Court).
8. Other judges of the Circuit Court who (being former Presidents of the Circuit Court) are ex-officio judges of the High Court, each according to priority of his or her appointment as President of the Circuit Court.
9. Other judges of the Circuit Court, other than judges of the District Court who (being a President or a former President of the District Court) are ex-officio judges of the Circuit Court, each according to priority of his or her appointment as a judge of the Circuit Court.
10. The President of the District Court (ex officio a judge of the Circuit Court).
11. Former Presidents of the District Court (ex officio judges of the Circuit Court) according to priority of his or her appointment as President of the District Court.
12. Other Judges of the District Court, each according to priority of his or her appointment as a judge of the District Court.

9.5.2 Solicitors

In Ireland there are two branches of the legal profession that can provide legal services; a division inherited from that existing in England and Wales.

Solicitors are the first contact point with the public and the ones who provide legal advice. They usually specialize in the preparation of cases for court and tend to work in private practice, although commercial and industrial organizations also employ solicitors, as do the Civil Service and the public sector generally.

The work of a solicitor varies from advising private clients on their personal and business lives (including such matters as marital problems or consumer complaints) to advising business clients on company matters. They also deal with all aspects of conveyancing (buying and selling of property, arranging loans, preparing title deeds, leases and other legal documents), wills, probate and administration of estates. They also have powers of litigation initiating or defending proceedings in the courts or by reference to arbitration or settling such claims or disputes 'out of court'.

Solicitors group under the Law Society of Ireland, the regulatory body of the profession in Ireland. It exercises statutory functions under the Solicitors Acts 1954 to 2008 in relation to the education, admission, enrolment, discipline and regulation of the solicitors' profession. The Law Society is governed by an elected Council, which is supported by a full-time executive led by the Director General.

9.5.3 Barristers

Barristers specialize in advocacy at the court and are not permitted to take instructions directly from the public, except in a small number of specific cases. Collectively, they are known as The Bar. Mirroring the London Inns of Court, the Honourable Society of King's Inns was established in Dublin to provide legal training for those wishing to practise at the Bar. Once they qualify as barristers and finish their pupillage, barristers become members of the Bar Council, the regulatory and representative body for barristers in Ireland. The Bar Council operates the Law Library, membership of which is compulsory for barristers, and which has become a metonym of the Bar Council itself, with the term being often used to refer to it.

Barristers provide specialized advice on a case, inform how it should be handled, draft the documents used in court to outline the case (the pleadings), draft the written submissions to the court when this is required and argue the case in court. The barrister and the solicitor tend to work together on individual cases, each covering a different but complementary aspect of the job of advising and representing their clients.

There is a distinction within the Bar between junior and senior counsel, depending on the years of practice and on the functions performed. Collectively, junior barristers are known as the Outer Bar and senior barristers are known as the Inner Bar. A junior counsel must practise for a minimum number of years, usually twelve, before being able to become a senior counsel. Promotion is not automatic and junior counsels must apply to the Chief Justice to become senior counsels. The actual appointment is made by the Government. Senior counsels are typically instructed in more serious or complex cases.

PART IV

Comparative Law for Legal Translators: From Theory to Practice

The final part of this volume offers a practical approach to the synergies between comparative law and legal translation.

Chapter 10 sets out to investigate the competences required to translate legal texts, and discusses whether legal translators should be trained as lawyers or as translators. A brief overview on how legal translators are currently being trained closes this section.

Chapter 11 adopts a didactic approach and, after presenting some of the strategies and techniques that can be applied in the translation of legal texts, moves on to provide illustrative examples and exercises that combine comparative law and legal translation.

CHAPTER 10

Training Legal Translators

In this chapter, we first outline the concept of translation competence and its application to the translation of legal texts. In the second section, the issue of whether legal translators should be trained as lawyers or as professional translators is raised. The third and last section focuses on the way in which legal translators are trained and on the role played by comparative law in their training, if any.

10.1 Translation competence in legal translation

From a training perspective, the study of comparative, and of national, law is justified as part of the translation competence which should be achieved by graduates in translation courses, not only as part of their cultural competence, in a broader sense, but also as part of their subject area or thematic competence. That is, translators should be aware of the fact that legal traditions are intimately related to the socio-cultural reality to which they belong and that law is not only part and parcel of the culture but also a (complex) discipline in itself.

It is not our intention here to defend or to define the concept of competence, as it has already been discussed by several authors both in a general context and in the framework of Translation Studies (PACTE 2000; González and Wagenaar 2003; Kelly 2005; EMT 2009). The objective is rather to identify the type of competence that is needed for the translation of legal texts. In this sense, we use the definition suggested by the Basic Skills, Entrepreneurship and Foreign Languages Working Group for the implementation of Education and Training 2010, as referred to by Kelly (2005: 33), which understands competence, 'to refer to a combination of skills, knowledge, aptitudes and attitudes, and to include disposition to learn as well as know-how'.

As for the competence that a translator should acquire, the differences between the various legal systems discussed in the previous chapters, compel legal translators to develop two main areas of competence. For our objective, we will first analyse two different proposals listing areas of competence desirable in graduates on translation courses (Kelly 2005; EMT 2009) and will later focus on legal translation competence models. According to Kelly (2005), translation competence is basically made up of seven areas of competence, as follows:

- Communicative and textual competence in at least two languages and cultures. This area covers both active and passive skills in the two languages involved, together with awareness of textuality and discourse, as well as textual and discourse conventions in the cultures involved.
- Cultural and intercultural competence. Culture refers not only to encyclopaedic knowledge of history, geography, institutions and so on of the two cultures involved, but also, and more particularly, values, myths, perceptions, beliefs, behaviours and textual representations of these. Awareness of issues of intercultural communication and translation as a special form thereof is also part of it.
- Subject area competence. Basic knowledge of subject areas in which the future translator will/may work, sufficient to allow comprehension of source texts and access to specialized documentation to solve translation problems.
- Professional and instrumental competence. Use of documentary resources of all kinds, terminological research, information management for these purposes, use of ICT tools for professional practice (word-processing, desktop publishing, data bases, internet, email ...) together with more traditional tools such as dictaphones. Basic notions for managing professional activity: contracts, tender, billing, tax, ethics, professional associations.

- Attitudinal or psycho-physiological competence. Self-concept, self-confidence, attention/concentration, memory, initiative.
- Interpersonal competence. Ability to work with other professionals involved in the actual translation process (translators, revisers, documentary researchers, terminologists, project managers, layout specialists), and other actors (clients, initiators, authors, users, subject area experts). Team work, negotiation skills, and leadership skills.
- Strategic competence. Organizational and planning skills, problem identification and problem-solving, monitoring, self-assessment and revision.

The European Master's in Translation (EMT) project, developed between 2006 and 2009, is a common frame of reference drawn up by the Directorate-General for Translation (DGT) of the European Commission. Set up to try and respond to the challenges arising from the new social and linguistic reality in Europe (expansion of markets, enlargement of the EU, lack of regulation of the profession, need for better working conditions and remuneration of translators, need for quality in training programmes), the EMT aims to establish a European reference framework for training programmes in translation which are coherent and of a high standard, comparable between centres of learning, and compatible with the demands of the international environment. For this purpose, a group of experts was set up in 2007 with a view to making specific proposals to implement a European reference framework for a Master's course in translation. One of their first results was the identification of six (interdependent) competences that should be acquired and mastered during training (EMT expert group 2009):

- Translation service provision competence.
- Language competence.
- Intercultural competence.
- Information mining competence.
- Thematic competence.
- Technological competence.

In both proposals, Kelly's and EMT's, all areas of competence are inter-dependent and must be combined to acquire translation competence. When training legal translators, as has been mentioned before, cultural/intercultural competence and subject area/thematic competence become essential in the following ways:

- Cultural/intercultural competence: legal systems must be under-stood as part of the culture of a given society, as the law evolves along with society, and translators must be aware of this social reality. For instance, some forty years ago it would have been impossible to think about legalizing marriage between same sex couples in countries such as Spain, where society had just gone through a rancid dictatorship. And yet, this legal institution has now been in place in Spain since 2005, thanks to a change in the mentality of the Spanish society and to a political shift in the Government.
- Subject area/thematic competence: to have the necessary thematic competence does not mean that a translator must know all aspects of a particular discipline, particularly in the first stages of training. This would be almost impossible for any translator working in any field and even more so for translators of legal texts, as they would need to have a thorough knowledge of the various legal systems with which they work. On the contrary, (trainee) translators must start by acquiring a basic knowledge of the area/s they work with and must also know how to access specialized documentation to solve the problems they may encounter. They should also be curious and prone to analysis and synthesis (Kelly 2005; EMT 2009). As translators specialize further with time, their expertise and familiarity with different concepts and institutions will broaden, which will in turn place them in a better position to successfully translate legal texts.

When dealing with legal texts, subject area/thematic competence refers not only to the thematic content of every branch of law or to the sources of law of every legal system, but also to aspects such as the organization of legal knowledge in the different legal systems, text typologies and textual conventions, terminology, legal language, and so on. All these aspects are highly influenced by culture, making cultural/intercultural and subject area/thematic competences to be strongly intertwined. Authors such as Prieto Ramos (2011: 11–12) bundles them together into a single one that he calls 'thematic and cultural competence', and which he defines as the 'knowledge of legal systems, hierarchy of legal sources, branches of law and main legal concepts; awareness of asymmetry between legal notions and structures in different legal traditions'. In addition to this thematic and cultural competence, the scholar proposes four other competences that complete his holistic model; the five of them comprising declarative and operative knowledge, to a greater or lesser extent:

- Strategic or methodological competence, which controls the application of the other skills and requires analysis of translation briefs, macro-contextualization and general work planning, identification of problems and implementation of transfer strategies (translation procedures), decision-making argumentation, self-assessment and quality control.
- Communicative and textual competence: linguistic, sociolinguistic and pragmatic knowledge, including awareness of linguistic variants, registers, specialized legal linguistic uses and legal genre conventions.
- Instrumental competence (documentation and technology): knowledge of specialized sources, information and terminology management, use of parallel documents, application of computer tools to translation.
- Interpersonal and professional management competence: teamwork, interaction with clients and other professionals, knowledge of legal framework for professional practice and fiscal obligations, deontological aspects.

The author also identifies other elements of legal science and legal linguistic knowledge that pervade legal translation competence:

- Scope of specialization: classification of legal genres (textual competence);
- Comparative legal linguistics: features of legal discourse in the source and the target languages and jurisdictions (communicative and textual competence);
- Documentation: specialized legal sources (instrumental competence);
- Professional practice: market conditions, associations and deontology issues in legal translation (interpersonal and professional management competence).

Šarčević (1997: 113–14) does not suggest a legal translation competence model as such, but insists on the (legal) competence needed by translators, which implies:

> [not only] in-depth knowledge of legal terminology, but also a thorough understanding of legal reasoning and the ability to solve legal problems, to analyse legal texts, and to foresee how a text will be interpreted and applied by the courts. [...] translators should also possess extensive knowledge of the target legal system as well. Moreover, drafting skills are required and a basic knowledge of comparative law and comparative methods.

Cao (2007) refers to legal translation proficiency and competence. For this author, legal translation proficiency refers to 'the ability to mobilize translation competence to perform legal translation tasks in the legal setting for intercultural and interlingual communication purposes' (*ibid.*: 39). She suggests a model of translation competence based in Wilss (1996: 57) description of general translational competence, formed by three aspects of knowledge-based behaviour: (1) the acquisition of knowledge, either in direct-experiential or in an indirect manner, (2) the storing of acquired knowledge in memory and (3) the reactivation of internalized knowledge, normally for multiple use either in a problem-solving setting or in automatized form. Consequently, Cao's (1996, 2007) model consists of three sets of variables interacting with one another in the context of situation: translational language competence, translational knowledge structures and translational strategic competence, which together constitute translation proficiency.

Piecychna (2013: 153) also develops a legal translation competence model, from a translational hermeneutics perspective, that sees the concepts of understanding and interpretation as pivotal elements of the four subcompetences that the author identifies:

> the proposed hermeneutical model is of both dynamic and circular character, which means that the specific subcompetences have so-called equal status and interrelate with each other. At the same time, each subcompetence is determined by the others, which simply indicates that they are complementary to each other. All these subcompetences form a global, hermeneutical, legal translation competence which is based on the translator as the central aspect of any translational process.

The following are the four subcompetences identified by the scholar in this model (*ibid.*: 153–4):

- Psychological subcompetence: self-reflection upon one's own skills and knowledge; reflection upon one's own cultural and social position as a legal translator; acceptance of one's own limitations and possible lack of skills or knowledge; acceptance of the subjective nature of the translational process; self-criticism; self-motivation; willingness to develop one's own knowledge; willingness to pursue a career as a legal translator; attitude towards translation work; being a responsible, curious, patient, creative, hard-working, diligent, methodical, devoted, and imaginative person; the ability to identify and solve problems with appropriate strategies and techniques; the ability to analyse and interpret texts.
- Thematic subcompetence: understanding and knowledge of the differences between various legal systems and cultures; the ability to compare various foreign legal systems with reference to the specificity of the translation task; understanding and knowledge of different subfields of law, such as civil law, criminal law, family law, international law, trade law, etc.; the ability to interpret and analyse a legal text.
- Textual subcompetence: knowledge of the typology of legal texts, legal genre conventions, legal terminology conceptualization, legal text register, legal text predicative mode and form; knowledge of formatting

conventions; knowledge of legal text function in specialist communication; the ability to interpret and analyse a legal text.
*   Linguistic subcompetence: knowledge of source and target languages
    in terms of grammar, lexis, stylistics, punctuation, spelling; knowledge
    of source and target legal language for specific purposes.

The author defends the idea that the elements forming the suggested model
are integrated and their configuration makes the legal translation process
different from other areas of specialized translation. This is supported by
the assertion that a legal translator must, first of all, understand a given
text and be able to position it within the particular situational context
with reference to both the source and target legal systems. To this end,
comparative law plays a central role for the successful accomplishment of
the translation task (*ibid.*).

The QUALETRA project (Quality in Legal Translation, <http://
www.eulita.eu/qualetra>) was developed in the framework of the European
Master's in Translation and financed by the EU. According to their website,
the expected overall result of the project was 'the conduction of transparent,
cost-effective criminal proceedings in the EU courts guaranteeing the rights
of suspected and accused persons as stipulated in Directive 2010/64/EU
and in the two Proposals for a Directive of the European Parliament and
of the Council'. The project also tackles legal translation competence and
suggests a model based on the EMT proposal, where the six competences
identified by the EMT are adapted or applied to the acquisition of legal
translation competence (Scarpa and Orlando 2014).

After having analysed several translation competence models, both
general and adapted to legal translation, we propose a model of legal translation competence based on the application of Kelly's (2005) model to
the particularities of legal translation. Below is the description of how the
seven areas of competence defined by Kelly, which become six areas in our
proposal, can be applied to legal translator training:

1. Communicative and textual competence. Legal translators must have
    a thorough knowledge of common/general and legal language in at
    least two legal cultures (or legal systems). Not only legal language

(terminology, phraseology, concepts) must be mastered, but also common language (how to write properly, ability to understand texts written in legalese). Textual conventions and text types. Legal discourse and different registers found in legal texts.

2. (Inter)cultural competence. Legal systems must be understood as part of the culture of a particular society, as the law evolves in the same way as society does. Knowledge of the social and political reality of a particular country or region. Traditions, customary law.

3. Subject area competence. Knowledge of legal families or traditions, legal systems, legal branches within the legal systems, sources of law, concepts, institutions, proceedings, substantive and procedural law, divergences between legal systems. The degree of knowledge will vary greatly depending on the competence and training stage of the translator. It is to be expected that trainees are not experts in the legal systems involved in the translation process, however they should have the skills necessary to access specialized documentation to solve translation problems.

4. Professional, interpersonal and instrumental competence. Kelly's professional and instrumental and interpersonal areas of competence have been merged into one as we consider that the skills needed in each of these areas are closely linked. This includes the use of specialized documentary sources, terminological research, information management, use of ICT tools, editing and post-editing. Use of parallel texts. Ability to work with other professionals involved in the translation process, including, but not limited to, experts in the legal field. Teamwork, negotiation skills, leadership skills. Basic notions for managing the professional activity.

5. Psychological competence. Labelled by Kelly as attitudinal or psychophysiological competence. Self-motivation, self-confidence to perform the tasks assigned adequately. Initiative. This area of competence is of particular importance for legal translators, who must work closely with legal professionals. Acceptance of one's own limitations.

6. Strategic competence. This is the organizational area of competence, the one that controls the implementation of the other areas of competence and their interdependence. Legal translators, like any other

translator, must have organizational and planning skills, must be able to self-assess and to revise their own work and must be able to identify problems and solve them. Problem identification and solving is often, but not only, related to the (inter)cultural and subject area competences as many of the challenges found in legal translation arise from the divergences between legal systems.

We have maintained the differentiation established by Kelly between cultural and intercultural competence (named (inter)cultural competence in our proposal) and the subject area competence as we consider that these two areas, though closely intertwined, must be differentiated. In our opinion, the former refers to the social and political reality of a country or region as a consequence of its historical and social development and evolution (as well as to legal traditions, how the law was formed, and customary law), while the latter basically alludes to the thematic content of law branches, institutions, concepts, proceedings and so on, which are at the base of substantive and procedural law in a given country or region. We consider that these two areas of competence are of key importance in legal translation, always in conjunction with the other areas. In our opinion, legal translators should be first trained to acquire the other areas of competence to later gain competence, gradually, in (inter)cultural and subject area issues specifically related to the legal field.

10.2 Should we train lawyer-linguists or legal translators?

After the above discussion, it seems clear that professional legal translators should be experts both in translation and, at least to a certain extent, in law. However, there is not always agreement as to what degree of legal knowledge is needed and one of the recurring issues in the field is whether we should train lawyers to translate legal texts or if, on the contrary, we should train translators who specialize in law.

Some voices defend a thorough and exhaustive training in legal aspects for professional translators, arguing on occasions that only someone who has legal training can translate legal texts. This is the case, for instance, at the European Court of Justice, where translators have to be lawyers; an approach defended by Meyer (in Wagner et al. 2002: 127), a legal reviser at the European Court of Justice, on the basis that the 'texts translated [...] are written in a particular way and with special legal concepts which only lawyers are able to understand fully and reproduce in their own language'. Along the same lines, but adopting a halfway solution, is Simonnaes (2013: 151), who affirms that: 'when having to compare pertinent legal institutions, one obviously cannot expect a translator who is not a lawyer to be able to apply the chosen method (i.e. a functional method of comparative law) with all its subtleties'. For this author, the ideal solution would be 'for the legal translator – a person with some knowledge of the pertinent legal domain – to work in a team with a lawyer where both would gain from being aware of the other's frame of reference' (*ibid.*).

Halfway positions are also held by authors such as Gémar (1982), who defends the existence of lawyer linguists in bilingual or plurilingual countries. These professionals would have a dual training in law and languages and would participate in the co-drafting of legislation or translate from one language into the other. This scholar does not defend the idea that legal translators should be exclusively trained as lawyers, but rather that they should be competent translators too (Gémar 1988). Other authors, like Sparer (2002), hold the position that lawyers do not necessarily make good translators and defend the idea of incorporating the legal domain in translator training programmes. In his opinion, it is not enough to be a lawyer to translate legal texts as these are, primarily, instruments of communication and it is not always obvious that lawyers have the appropriate communication skills that guarantee an understandable target text. This opinion is also shared by Lavoie (2003), who argues that legal translators do not need to be fully trained as lawyers and proposes that they study translation and specialize in the legal field.

Prieto Ramos (2011: 13) underlines the need to understand and produce legal translations with 'lawyer-linguist' eyes, which means that 'a legal translator should be familiar with legal reasoning, interpretation rules, legal

phraseology, legal sources used by jurists, and legal structures and procedures with reference to particular types of legal systems'. According to this
author, 'an ideal legal translator should be a lawyer-linguist, a professional
able to connect legal and specialized linguistic skills, and, consequently,
a person who should possess very good knowledge and skills within the
scope of both law and linguistics and, consequently, legal text interpretation abilities' (*ibid.*). He then moves on to query the degree of expertise
in legal topics that translators should have: 'If we agree that legal translators should be experts in law and be familiar with at least one field of the
domain, be it civil law, criminal law, family law, etc., we should first try to
determine the extent of the knowledge that is necessary of both source and
target legal systems' (*ibid.*). The scholar supports (legal) translator training
as opposed to (exclusive) legal training and asserts that:

> generalizations according to which law graduates are better candidates for legal
> translation than translation graduates are rather simplistic. Assuming that legal
> translation reasonably requires postgraduate specialization, the starting level in each
> subcompetence to be developed can vary enormously depending on the individual
> profile. In broad terms, however, those with a (national) legal background can be
> expected to have a very strong thematic competence (even if often lacking essential
> comparative legal components), but also important deficiencies in key linguistic, tex-
> tual and strategic competences; whereas the reverse might be the case for translation
> graduates. In any event, the ultimate challenge within the interdiscipline would be
> to produce highly competent legal translators through comprehensive legal transla-
> tion training rather than presuming expert performance only from a double parallel
> qualification in translation and law (*ibid.*: 19).

In our opinion, professional translators should ideally be experts in translation and in law, both in the source and in the target legal systems they work
with. In this sense, we agree with Prieto Ramos (*ibid.:* 13) that:

> the deeper the knowledge of legal subjects, the more confident the translator can
> feel when dealing with legal content issues during analysis and transfer stages of
> translation; and, as the argument reasonably goes, those trained in both translation
> and law potentially make the best legal translators.

However, we consider that legal translators do not necessarily have to be
trained as lawyers, mainly for two reasons. First of all, legal training at

universities usually involves knowledge of just one legal system (and some aspects of international law) and teaching normally focuses on the needs of professional lawyers, which are not necessarily the same as those faced by translators of legal texts. Secondly, we share the opinion of authors such as Šarčević (1994, 1997), who consider that a high degree of professionalism can only be attained if legal translators have been trained in both law and translation. Yet, this does not necessarily mean having to pursue two university degrees as lawyers and translators, and it would be more realistic to offer interdisciplinary legal translator training programmes into which law and translation courses are integrated.

Of course, graduates in both disciplines would make ideal legal translators as it is to be expected that they are competent in all the legal translation competence areas, even if their knowledge of source and target legal systems might be unbalanced. Nonetheless, translator training alone can also produce excellent legal translators. As it may be difficult to completely develop (inter)cultural and subject area competences in translation courses, it is important that the other competences are successfully acquired by translators-to-be. These two areas of competence can then be improved gradually within professional translation practice and further education, such as postgraduate courses in legal aspects.

10.3 The training of legal translators

Once identified the areas of competence needed by legal translators and discussed the qualifications required, we will now briefly analyse how legal translators are actually trained and the role, if any, played by comparative law in the training of legal translators.

The second half of the twentieth century witnessed the increase of institutions specializing in the training of translators and interpreters though the interest for legal translation education can be traced back to some decades before. In this sense, Caminade and Pym (1998: 281) indicate that the Copenhagen Business School started training legal translators in

1921 and the Paris Institut de Droit Comparé in 1931. Nowadays, translation is an academic discipline delivered in different ways in the various
countries where it constitutes part of the university curriculum. Within
the European context, some educational institutions offer undergraduate
degrees on translation under the wider umbrella titles of applied or modern
languages, and in some nations translation degrees are part of the provision offered by business and administration schools. Other countries, such
as Italy or Spain, offer translation specific undergraduate degrees, where
more emphasis is placed on building up translation specific competences.
Students usually learn how to translate different types of texts belonging
to different fields and disciplines and they start developing subject area
competence along with the other areas of competence. In some cases, an
interdisciplinary approach is followed and students enrol on specialized
courses in a particular field, such as law, that lead to a semi-specialization in
that subject area. Outside of Europe, the scenario is similar and it is often
the case that translation is taught at postgraduate level once students have
acquired basic transferable competences at undergraduate level. Training
in legal translation is also varied and takes different forms depending on
the academic culture of the country or on the institution in which it is
offered. In the United States, France or the United Kingdom, to name but
a few, legal translation is normally studied at postgraduate level, during a
one- or two-year Master's programme.

This educational scenario is constantly changing, due mainly to the
academic reforms implemented in some countries, particularly in those
which belong to the European Higher Education Area. In recent years,
undergraduate translation degrees have been redesigned and now aim
mainly at training generalist translators. As a consequence, an increasing number of translation programmes are being offered at postgraduate
level in many universities around the world. In some cases, these are general programmes in translation designed for students coming from other
disciplines, but more frequently universities offer programmes centred
on specialized translation, such as legal, financial, medical or audiovisual translation. MA programmes in legal translation normally adopt an
interdisciplinary approach and often include one or more subjects on law
and/or on comparative law, where students learn about the importance

for translation of comparing concepts, institutions, rules or proceedings. When specific subjects on (comparative) law are not included, comparative methodology is taught through the practice of translation in regular legal translation classes.

As expressed in these pages, we are of the opinion that the acquisition and development of the subject area competence in legal translation should be done not through the study of national law but through research in comparative law instead. However, the role of comparative law is still a secondary one in most university programmes, both in translation and law, as it is not considered a discipline as such. A notable exception to this state of affairs can be found in Italian universities, where comparative law is generally studied as part of the curriculum. It is also possible nowadays to find postgraduate courses on the study of comparative law from a legal perspective.

CHAPTER II

Legal Translation in the Classroom

As discussed in Chapter 1, the interaction between comparative law and legal translation arises from the fact that, due to the divergences between legal systems, translators need to firstly understand legal concepts (terminology, institutions, proceedings ...) from at least two different legal systems and then translate them from one system to another. This chapter now centres on analysing how comparative law can be a useful tool in the practice of translating legal texts. Rather than focusing on legislative texts or any other text type within one single legal system, that do not pose serious translation challenges as they usually refer to the same reality albeit in two different languages, we will concentrate instead on the transfer of legal concepts, institutions, rules or proceedings which form a part of different legal systems, even if those different legal systems coexist in one single country. Translations of texts will not be offered, but we will analyse different strategies and applications of comparative law in the translation of legal texts.

We will start by describing some of the strategies and techniques that we consider essential for the translation of legal texts and will later provide some examples of how comparative law can be used in day-to-day translation practice. Finally, a battery of exercises is put forward in the hope that they will assist in the training of legal translators.

11.1 The translation process: Macro-comparison vs micro-comparison and strategies in legal translation

Two main stages can be differentiated when applying comparative law to the translation of legal documents: (1) the process consisting of the acquisition of the (inter)cultural and subject area competences and (2) the process leading to the creation of a new text. For our purposes, the first stage can be divided into two different methodologies: macro- and micro-comparison (see Chapter 1). The macro-comparison of the different legal systems involved in the translation process will allow the translator to acquire the background or basic (inter)cultural and subject area competences. Once trainees grasp the rudiments, similarities and differences of the legal systems at play, they have to carry out an in-depth analysis of legal terms, institutions, documents or proceedings, usually on an individual basis for every translation brief. In this process of micro-comparison, students may be faced with one or more of the following situations:

1.   the legal concept, institution, rule or proceeding analysed can be found in both legal cultures;
2.   the legal concept, institution, rule or proceeding analysed can be found in one culture but only partially in the other;
3.   the legal concept, institution, rule or proceeding analysed can be found in one culture but not in the other.

Incongruence is one of the main problems encountered in the translation of legal texts and one of the worries for scholars has been to find appropriate equivalents between different realities in two or more legal systems. Although equivalence has been the object of study of many academic works (Hickey 1993; Franzoni de Moldavski 1996; Šarčević 1997), it is still a concept on which authors do not fully agree. Franzoni de Moldavski (1996), for instance, questions whether or not equivalence is possible and, if so, she wonders whether this criterion is the only valid one or the desirable one in every case. Hickey (1993: 66), in his article about equivalence in legal translation, asserts that 'a translator's task is to produce a target text that will cause on the reader of the translation approximately the same effect as the original caused on the readers for which it was intended'.

Contrary to Hickey's position, the functionalist theory gives priority to the adequacy of the target text to the function or aim of the new text within the target culture and it is along these lines that we draw our suggested translation methodology. Translators may decide to apply different strategies depending on the translation brief (Nord 1997), the communicative situation and the particular legal concept they are translating. In some cases, the aim is to find equivalents for certain source concepts, whilst in others they may need to explain a legal concept, not just because it can be only found in one of the two cultures, but also because the particular communicative situation might call for a different translation solution to the one adopted on other occasions.

When the objective is to find an equivalent for a legal concept, Šarčević (1997) proposes a method based on the studies undertaken by the *Internationales Institut für Rechts- und Verwaltungssprache* in Berlin, of functionalist inspiration (Reiss and Vermeer 1996; Nord 1997), and according to which terms can be dissected into principal and incidental characteristics. In this approach, the comparison of the characteristics of different terms belonging to different legal cultures offers the potential of helping with the identification of equivalent terms within different legal systems. A practical application of this methodology to the translation of terms related to children guardianship between Spain and England and Wales is presented in Section 11.2.1.

The methodology we suggest for the translation of legal texts is based on the following assumptions:

1. It is of utmost importance to know or, at least, to be familiar with the legal cultures involved in the translation process.
2. Translation of a particular text is influenced by the translation brief, the communicative situation, the purpose of the translation, the type of text, the context and the elements of the text.
3. Finding equivalents in the target language is not always possible or necessary and translators will have to resort to various translations techniques depending on the context.

As for the first assumption, it has already been discussed that law, as a national or even regional phenomenon, requires the translator to have a grasp, or at least to be familiar with, the legal systems involved in the translation process. Finding translators who are specialists in the two (or more) legal systems at play may prove difficult but they should at least have a general understanding of the topic and the necessary competence to explore the different areas of law with which they may need to work.

Translators should not translate a text without knowing the intended readership and the purpose that is supposed to serve. As the minimum requirements of a translation brief, they allow the translator to adapt the target product to the client and the reader. The purpose of the translation, the potential background knowledge of the reader, the text type, the context in which the translation is produced and will be read, and the elements of the text, will influence the translation process. Translation strategies may (and will definitely) vary if professionals have to translate a legislative text to be applied in the different countries of the European Union or if they have to translate a birth certificate from Senegal for someone who is trying to regularize their situation in Spain. In the first case, we can expect that EU law is homogeneous for all member states and most concepts have been standardized, which should make translation an 'easier' task, as the search for equivalents is not necessary. Yet, this assertion must be nuanced as it is often the case that legal transplants and legal harmonization can create difficult translation challenges and reference to national legal concepts must be repeatedly made in EU legislation. In the second case, Senegal and Spain are two countries with a very different background and social and legal reality. This particular text type, and the purpose it serves, will call for a different translation strategy. The translation will be 'official', in the sense that it will be presented to the authorities in Spain, but the focus or reference will not be Spanish law, but Senegalese law instead. Ultimately, the translated text must be understood by the reader, i.e. the Spanish authorities, and serve its purpose. The first example is illustrative of covert (House 1977) or instrumental (Nord 1991) translation, as the target text enjoys the status of an original text in the target culture. This translation is not marked pragmatically as such but could have been created in its own right. In the second case, we have an example of overt (House 1977) or documentary

(Nord 1991) translation, that is, a target text whose origin is clear and does not stand as if it were a second original, it informs the reader about certain aspects of the source text and its communicative situation.

In some cases, it is not only impossible to find a full equivalent for a given concept, but it could be inappropriate for the translation brief and the communicative situation. In the previous example of the translation of a Senegalese birth certificate into Spanish to regularize the situation of a Senegalese citizen in Spain, some concepts will probably need to be explained and the search for equivalents will not be sufficient. That may be the case, for instance, of the Senegalese institutions, which, being so culturally bound to the country, do not have an equivalent in Spain and contriving one would not serve the translation purpose as it may be misleading for the reader. On these occasions, when an equivalent concept does not exist or, even if it exists, its use is not appropriate, two potential options are possible. Firstly, the provision of an explanation of the particular concept, taking into account the communicative situation and the purpose of the translation; what could be called a descriptive translation. Secondly, the translator can offer a literal translation of the term – linguistic equivalence – if this is transparent enough and does not lead to any misunderstandings. An example could be the translation of the English 'Court of Appeal' for *Tribunal de Apelación* in Spanish.

Depending on the legal cultures involved in the translation process, other techniques may also be useful, such as transcription, borrowing or adaptation (Borja Albi 2000), though some of the other strategies suggested by this scholar (i.e. creation of neologisms and naturalization) should be discouraged in the day-to-day work of translators. Harvey (2000) has also written on the translation techniques used in the legal field, with a special focus on culture-bound terms, and mentions these four: functional equivalence, formal – or linguistic – equivalence, transcription or borrowing and descriptive or self-explanatory translation. The following sections offer examples of how different translation techniques are applied depending on the context, the text type and the communicative situation.

11.2 Application of comparative law to legal translation practice: Terminology

In this section two examples on how comparative law can be applied to the translation of legal terms are discussed. Firstly, the methodology developed by the Berlin Institute mentioned above is applied to a series of terms in a quest for equivalence. The second example shows how other techniques, discussed in Section 11.1, can be used when the translation brief, the communicative situation and the source terms themselves do not allow the translator to use equivalent terms.

11.2.1 The search for equivalence

The methodology developed by the Berlin *Internationales Institut für Rechts- und Verwaltungssprache* mentioned above has been applied to the analysis of terms used in the field of child guardianship (Soriano-Barabino 2002b). In this study, a comparison between three terms belonging to the Spanish civil code and regulating different situations of guardianship are compared to three terms also regulating different situations of guardianship in England and Wales and belonging to the English Children Act 1989, which was later updated by the Children Act 2004 and is currently in force in England and Wales.

The coupled terms selected for the comparison were 'guardian' and *tutor*, 'guardian ad litem' and *defensor judicial*, and 'wardship' and *tutela automática* (taken over by a public institution). All of them were dissected into essential and accidental characteristics and then compared to each other.[1]

---

1   According to Cabré (1995), essential characteristics are those that define the essence of a term and cannot be avoided in the definition of the term, whilst accidental characteristics add elements irrelevant for the description.

The aspects selected in order to dissect terms into essential and accidental characteristics were: (1) the object of the institution or figure, as indicated above; (2) who is or are the person or persons under protection in each case; (3) who is eligible to exert protection; (4) who can ask the authorities or the court to establish the protection institution, and (5) how this institution is established.

For the two first coupled terms we found that the object of both institutions is to appoint one person to exert parental responsibility towards a child who has no parents or whose parents do not exert it over him or her. The persons eligible to exert protection in both cases, 'guardianship' and *tutor*, are found to be similar in both cases. As for who can ask the authorities to establish these institutions and how they are established, even if some minor differences can be found, these respond mainly to the divergences in functioning in the two legal cultures more than to any other reason.

A child is again the person who can be placed under protection in both cases for the pair 'guardian ad litem' and *defensor judicial*. The persons eligible to be appointed as 'guardian ad litem' or *defensor judicial* are also the same in both legal systems and so is the procedure to establish these institutions. The main difference between them lies in who can ask the authorities or the court to determine child protection.

The only similarities found in the comparison between 'wardship' and *tutela automática* (taken over by a public institution) were the main task of both institutions to protect children and the fact that protection is automatically taken over by a public body. The conclusions reached are the following:

- The terms 'guardian' and *tutor* could be considered functional equivalents as the essential characteristics of both terms are coincident, even if some of the accidental characteristics differ.
- The terms 'guardian ad litem' and *defensor judicial* share most essential characteristics but not all of them. Both terms could be considered partially equivalent and the decision to use one to translate the other should be taken by the translator according to the translation brief and the communicative situation.

- Lastly, the terms 'wardship' (inherent jurisdiction of court with respect to children) and *tutela automática* only share a few essential characteristics and cannot be considered to be functionally equivalent.

This is a practical application of micro-comparison through which the examination of the essential and accidental characteristics of the various terms provides translators with a thorough understanding of the legal terms and the background surrounding them. In addition, it allows them to go beyond the linguistic term and grasp the sense implicit in the legal concepts to find the appropriate equivalents in the target culture (if they exist) for the concepts of the source culture.

11.2.2 *When equivalence is not the aim*

Sometimes the translation brief calls for the implementation of translation techniques other than the search for equivalents, either because there are no functional equivalents for the concept or institution or because the existing one 'does not work' in a particular communicative situation. This may be the case when translating culture-bound terms, defined by Harvey (2000: 2) as 'concepts, institutions and personnel which are specific to the SL culture'. Indeed, institutions such as jurisdictional bodies belonging to a given legal system may differ so greatly from other systems that it may be impossible to provide appropriate equivalents. And, even if we could find a partially equivalent institution we should be careful as the effect caused on the reader could be misleading and not the one intended.

For our example we have chosen the French courts in charge of criminal matters, namely *cour d'assises*, *tribunal correctionnel* and *tribunal de police*, and have assumed that the translation brief and communicative situation call for a descriptive translation. The first step would then be to establish the main characteristics of the courts, as discussed in Chapter 4:

> *Cour d'assises*: formed by professional judges and by a jury of lay people. It is competent to try *crimes*, major offences or serious crimes, and offences connected with them.

Tribunal correctionnel: competent to try *délits*, i.e. major offences committed within its territorial jurisdiction.

Tribunal de police: lowest criminal court that deals with minor offences.

Based on this general description, it is possible to suggest a descriptive translation for each of them:

Cour d'assises: [French] criminal court that deals with most major offences or serious crimes and tries by jury.

Tribunal correctionnel: [French] criminal court that deals with crimes of less importance [than the ones tried by the *cour d'assises*].

Tribunal de police: [French] criminal court that deals with minor offences.

This explanatory technique keeps the source culture as the reference of the translated concept and does not call for a search for equivalents. This approach is most fruitful when the translation brief requires that the reference to the source term is not lost, as it would be interesting for the reader to know the actual term in the source language and culture. Harvey (2000: 6) praises this technique as 'it has the advantage of being transparent and easy to memorize. It is appropriate in a wide variety of contexts where a formal equivalent [linguistic equivalent] is considered insufficiently clear'.

11.3 Application of comparative law to legal translation practice: Textology

Asymmetry between legal systems can be found not only in terminological issues but also at textual level, as legal texts may be organized differently in different legal cultures. The example in the table below shows the main similarities and discrepancies that can be found between the official permanent employment contracts for household workers issued by the Spanish and French authorities (see Table 7).[2] The main difference to be noted is their formal appearance. In the case of the French contract on the left, it follows the same standard structure as any other contract in France, whereas employment contracts in Spain respond to a highly standardized convention that uses boxes to be completed and maintains the references to the public employment services, differentiating them from other similar documents such as purchasing contracts, for instance:

Table 7: Comparison between permanent employment contracts in France and Spain

Contrat de travail à durée indéterminée (salarié du particulier employeur) [Fixed term contract (for housekeeping services)]	Contrato de trabajo indefinido (del servicio de hogar familiar) [Fixed term contract (for housekeeping services)]
Entre l'employeur: [information about the employer].	Information about the employer.
Et le ou la salarié(e): [information about the employee].	Information about the employee.
	Identification of the legal representative for the employee (if applicable).
	DECLARAN [the parties state that they have the legal capacity required to enter into the contract].
Les termes du contrat: [information about the applicable legislation, terms and conditions:].	CLÁUSULAS [Terms and conditions:]

2   Models of official permanent employment contracts in France and Spain can be found as appendixes at the end of this book. Appendix 1 shows an official model of *Contrat de travail à durée indéterminée – Salarié du Particulier employeur* (<www.cesu.urssaf. fr/cesweb/pdf/contrat.pdf>) and Appendix 2 shows the official model approved by the Spanish Ministry of Employment and Social Security for a *Contrato de trabajo indefinido del servicio del hogar familiar* (<www.empleo.gob.es/es/portada/servicio hogar/modelos/Mod-PE-171.pdf>).

Contrat de travail à durée indéterminée (salarié du particulier employeur) [Fixed term contract (for housekeeping services)]	Contrato de trabajo indefinido (del servicio de hogar familiar) [Fixed term contract (for housekeeping services)]
1. Organismes de retraite et prévoyance [applicable institutions for retirement].	PRIMERA. [Type of employment and place of work].
2. Date d'entrée [date of entry].	SEGUNDA. [Number of hours worked per week, month or year].
3. Lieu habituel de travail [work address].	TERCERA. [Number of working hours, if applicable].
4. Nature de l'emploi [type of employment].	CUARTA. [Length of contract].
5. Description du poste [description of memployment].	QUINTA. [Provisions for night shifts or in-house nights].
6. Niveau de qualification [qualification].	SEXTA. [Salary].
7. Horaires de travail hebdomadaire [working hours per week].	SÉPTIMA. [Holidays].
8. Jour de repos hebdomadaire [day off per week].	OCTAVA. [Information about tax obligations].
9. Jours fériés [bank holidays].	NOVENA. [Applicable legislation].
10. Rémunération [salary].	DÉCIMA. [Legal provisions regarding communication to the public employment services].
11. Indemnités kilométriques [payment for kilometres if the employee uses own car].	
12. Prestations en nature [fringe benefits].	
13. Date de paiement de la rémunération [date of salary payment].	
14. Congés payés [paid holidays].	
15. Clauses particulières [additional terms and conditions].	CLÁUSULAS ADICIONALES [additional terms and conditions].
16. Number of copies of contract.	Number of copies of contract.
Signatures of the parties and date.	Date and signatures of the parties.

As can be noted in the table above, the differences are not only structural but also in terms of the information provided. As far as the structure is concerned, these are the main differences to be noted:

- The information about the employer and the employee in the French contract appear as paragraphs, whereas in the Spanish contract there are boxes to be completed.
- The French contract includes a digit before each term and condition, whilst in the Spanish contract the numbers before each term and condition are written in full, in capital letters.
- In the Spanish contract, there are terms (*'DECLARAN'*, *'CLÁUSULAS'*) that help to divide the contract into clearly differentiated parts.

Content-wise, the French contract includes more detailed information than its Spanish counterpart, with the following main differences:

- In the French contract there is information about the competent institutions for retirement.
- The French contract includes more detailed information about holidays and days off.
- The Spanish contract specifically states that the parties have the required legal capacity to enter into the contract.
- The information regarding working hours is much more detailed in the French contract.
- The French contract establishes a detailed list of household employment types, the description of the post and the qualifications of the employee.

Differences in structure and content are bound to exist between the same text types in different legal systems, even if these are as relatively close as the French and the Spanish ones. Translators must be aware of these dissimilarities if they are to perform successfully, though their final decision on the structure and the information that should appear in the target text will ultimately depend on the translation brief and the communicative situation of the source and target texts.

Related to textology is the fact that legal systems may also differ as far as proceedings are organized and it is possible to find documents that exist in one legal system for a particular proceeding but are non-existent in another legal system. An example is provided by Calvo Encinas (2002), when she analyses the documents used for divorce proceedings in Ireland and Spain following the methodology developed by the Berlin *Internationales Institut für Rechts- und Verwaltungssprache* (see Section 11.1). Her conclusion is that the Irish 'divorce decree' and the Spanish *sentencia de divorcio* can be considered to be functionally equivalent as their main effect is the same, i.e. they both dissolve the marriage. However, there is no equivalent under Spanish law for the Irish Certificate pursuant to Section 6 of the Family Law (Divorce) Act 1996, former Form No. 9 of the Circuit Family Law Court 1996, and currently Form 37D of Circuit Court Rules, which reads as follows:

> the Plaintiff/Defendant has been fully advised in relation to alternative forms of matrimonial dispute resolution to include marriage guidance counselling, mediation, separation agreements and other forms of matrimonial litigation.

In this document, the solicitor acting for the respondent, currently defendant, certifies that s/he has discussed with the respondent the possibility of reconciliation with the applicant, currently plaintiff, has given the respondent the possibility of mediation and has discussed with the respondent the possibility of negotiating a separation deed or separation agreement with the applicant. This document, as Calvo Encinas (2002) states, was a response by the Irish legislator to appease the differences in opinion of the Irish society, in which many citizens were not at ease with the idea of divorce. In Spain, on the other hand, the *abogados* do not have the obligation to invite the parties of a divorce to reconcile or to go to mediation, although they could of course do so, and therefore there is no document provision for this.

These examples illustrate how a prior analysis of concepts, institutions, texts and proceedings is necessary in order to find a potentially suitable translation, according to a given brief and communicative situation, for some terms or institutions belonging to a particular legal system or to provide translators with a conceptual organization of texts and proceedings which will orientate them towards the best way to approach a translation and the techniques to be activated. Of course, this analysis can only be performed through the comparison of legal concepts, institutions, texts and proceedings.

11.4 From theory to practice

As indicated at the beginning of this chapter, translation being a practical activity, it is fundamental that comparative law be taught also in a practical way. Based on experience, we believe that the best way to train translators-to-be in how to apply comparative law to their daily routine would be first to give them the basic legal theoretical rudiments and later show them how to apply theory to practice. Acquiring basic legal knowledge can be achieved by putting professional and instrumental competence into practice (particularly through documentary research) but the comparison of legal systems, though a fundamental part of the process, is not translation itself and, therefore, is not the aim of legal translators. The key point is that trainees learn how to apply the theory to their translation process and final product.

In this section, we propose a series of useful activities for translators, who need to be able to understand legal texts, grasp the effects and implications of legal concepts and produce new texts according to a given translation brief and communicative situation. The exercises focus on the development of the (inter)cultural and subject area competences and are mainly aimed at future translators of legal texts, though they can also be used by trainers of legal translators and by professional translators who want to specialize in this field. The list of tasks is not exhaustive and can be taken as an example from which new exercises could be developed. Scholars such as Dullion (2015) suggest the staggering of exercises in six stages, but for this section three stages have been considered more appropriate, according to the student training stage: awareness raising, identification and recognition of translation problems related to comparative law, and comparison itself. The principles guiding the design and selection of exercises are the following:

1. To use comparative law as a tool for legal translation.
2. To show the different aspects involved in the interaction between legal translation and comparative law; a principle also underlined by Dullion (2015: 12) in her proposal of exercises aimed at 'mobilising comparative law for translating'.
3. To apply a functionalist approach to the translation of legal texts.
4. To focus on translation problems that derive from comparative law.
5. To offer an integrated approach, where different aspects are taken into account, such as asymmetries between legal systems, textology, terminology, legal language, and the like.

Finally, the exercises are divided into two broad groups within each stage: (1) general exercises, to be applied to any language and legal combination, and (2) culture-bound exercises, specific to the legal systems covered in this volume. It goes without saying that trainees can be asked to read relevant literature to guide them during the implementation of the exercises.

11.4.1 Awareness raising: General exercises

As legal systems do not necessarily share the same textual conventions, being aware of the differences is important for translators, not only in order to produce a text that meets the expectations of the target reader, but also to become familiar with the cultures involved in the transfer process. The following four exercises aim to raise awareness about the different textual conventions.

(a) Same text type

> Look for the same text type (for example, birth certificates, sale contracts,
> bills of exchange, last wills and testaments) in your source and target
> legal cultures and analyse the documents from a macro-structural point
> of view. Identify similarities and differences and compare the results. Try
> to find more than one example of each text typology so that the conclu-
> sions reached can be generalized.

(b) Different text types

> Look for some text types in your source and target legal cultures that
> appear to be different but are used for the same legal purpose.

(c) Textual asymmetries

> Look for a variety of text types that exist in the source legal culture but
> which cannot be found in the target culture. For example, in France
> there is an administrative document called *Demande de prime de démé-*
> *nagement* [Application for a bonus to move] that can be used to apply
> for financial help to change one's residence when certain conditions are
> met. This document is quite unique to the French system and does not
> seem to exist in many other cultures.

(d) Classification of legal texts

The vast array of legal texts in the market makes it difficult for translators
to fully grasp the nuances of all the documents. Asking students to clas-
sify legal texts helps them to become familiar with a variety of text types
belonging to different legal cultures. Various classifications can be used and
applied to this exercise, either on their own or combined.

> Look for legal texts belonging to your source and target cultures and
> classify them according to their subject area and function. Follow the
> categories proposed by Reiss and Vermeer (1996) and Hatim and Mason
> (1990) for different text functions.

11.4.2 Awareness raising: Culture-bound exercises

(a) Textual asymmetries (Spain as the source legal system)

Differences between legal systems are not just found in the use of terminology, but also in textual conventions. Texts with the same function in two legal systems may be organized in different ways and translators should be able to recognize these conventions in order to fully and correctly understand the source text and to produce a text that complies with the requirements of the translation brief.

A Spanish final judgement [*sentencia*] is made up of the following parts:

Encabezamiento – Antecedentes de Hecho – Fundamentos de Derecho – Fallo

Find out how the different elements of a final judgement are structured in your target legal system and decide how this different organization is, or may be, relevant for your translation brief.

(b) Textual asymmetries (Germany and Spain as source and target legal systems)[3]

Some legal texts have a similar content, but a different structure, in two legal systems. In cases like this, translators should decide the structure to be followed and the final decision will have to be taken in accordance with the translation brief and the communicative situation.

Compare the structure of the final judgment in German and in Spanish:

URTEIL	SENTENCIA
Rubrum	*Encabezamiento*
Tenor	*Hechos*
Tatbestand	*Fundamentos de Derecho*
Entscheidungsgründe	*Fallo*

---

3   Exercises dealing with the German legal system have been designed by Rafael A. Zambrana Kuhn in collaboration with the author, and those dealing with the Italian legal system have been designed by Angela Carpi in collaboration with the author.

(c)   Textual asymmetries (England and Wales, the United States and Ireland)

Professionals can also be faced with legal texts that share identical function and content in most legal systems, such as birth or death certificates. However their textual conventions may vary from one legal culture to another, and even within the same country. This exercise helps to raise awareness about the dissimilarities found in textual conventions between different cultures, even when these cultures share a common language, as is the case of the legal systems of England and Wales, the US and Ireland.

Find birth certificates from England and Wales, the United States and Ireland and compare them. Indicate the similarities and dissimilarities that you can find between them in terms of the use of terminology and textual conventions.

(d)   Intralingual translation (Spain as source or target legal system)

This exercise aims at raising awareness among future translators, using the Spanish legal system as one of their working legal systems, of the linguistic complexity of legalese and encourages them to use plain legal language.

Re-write the following text in plain Spanish. Identify the legal terms that have a different meaning in general language and in legal language and explain their meaning:

Establecido el usufructo universal a favor del cónyuge supérstite y acaecida la preterición no intencional de un heredero forzoso, la legítima de éste se ve perjudicada por el legado universal y vitalicio a favor de la viuda, de donde procede anular la institución de heredero hecha por el testador a favor de dos herederos forzosos (hijos matrimoniales), reducir por inoficioso el legado a favor del cónyuge viudo y abrir la sucesión intestada del haber hereditario restante. (Part of a judgement by the Spanish *Tribunal Supremo*, 30 January 1995)

(e) Historical references (Germany as source or target legal system)

Translators often have to deal with historical references in legal texts that might have an accepted translation, established throughout history and which has to be maintained.

Consider the term *Reich*:

A standard translation for *Reich* would be *Empire*. However when we speak of the German Empire, we are only referring to the period under Bismarck's government, i.e. between 1871 and 1918. Then again, Wilhelm II is usually referred to as the *Kaiser*, rather than the Emperor. However the term *III Reich* is never translated but always maintained as such. Thus, for the translation of *Reichsgesetz* we need to know if that particular law was passed under Bismarck's government (Imperial Act) or during the III Reich (Act of the Reich).

(f) Procedural asymmetries (Italy as source legal culture)

Differences between legal systems can also be found in proceedings. In particular, a proceeding can take a certain number of steps in a legal system and follow different ones in another system, even if the purpose or the final consequence is the same in both systems. In this exercise, students are asked to work with documents that belong to a complete divorce proceeding in Italy.

Find out what a *separazione giudiziale* and a *separazione consensuale* are in Italy. They belong to a specific procedure and are necessary in order to obtain a divorce declaration. Do they also exist in your target legal system? How would you translate *procedimento di separazione* in your target legal system? And the term *separazione con addebito*?

(g) Procedural asymmetries (England and Wales as source legal culture)

This exercise, also on procedural asymmetries, focus on a document that belongs to a divorce proceeding in England and Wales but that does not exist in all legal systems.

Find out what a 'decree *nisi*' and a 'decree absolute' are in England and Wales. Do these texts exist in your target legal system? How would you translate 'decree *nisi*' into the language of your target legal system? And 'decree absolute'?

(h) Different meanings for the same terms in different legal systems (England and Wales, the United States and Ireland as target legal systems)

Due to the different cultural and historical evolution of legal systems, it is reasonably common to find the same term with a different meaning in another legal culture, even if the language is the same. Translators need to be aware of the link existing between a particular legal language and a specific legal culture and they must bear in mind the reader of the target text. As concepts can be very intimately linked to their culture, on occasions it is necessary to resort to a term with no (legal) cultural meaning.

Compare the meaning of the four sets of terms below and decide on the lexical item that you would use for your translation into English in the situations stated. Justify your decision.

Certified Public Accountant, Chartered Accountant and Licensed Accountant:
– If the reader is an English lawyer
– If the reader is a Swedish businessman

Law Clerk and Legal Executive:
– If the reader is an Irish law student
– If the reader is an English law student

Answer and Defence:
– If the reader is a United States lawyer
– If the reader is an English barrister

Certificate of title and land certificate:
– If the reader is a United States lawyer
– If the reader is an English solicitor

> Find out the meaning of the following terms in the English, US and
> Irish legal systems:
> – Attorney
> – Counsel
> – Charge certificate
> – Docket

11.4.3 Identification and recognition of translation problems: General exercises

(a) Identifying translation problems

Translators must be able to recognize translation problems before produc-
ing the target text and this exercise helps to identify them so that they can
be analysed and solved during the transfer process.

> Identify all the legal terms or expressions that may be a translation prob-
> lem in a given source text. Offer ways to solve the problem in each case,
> i.e. do not offer a translation solution for each particular term or expres-
> sion, but rather consider the kind of documentary research that would
> help solve the translation problems.

(b) Terminology

The following exercise will help students to create a tool that they can use
during their translation practice, encourages them to avoid using bilingual
dictionaries, and invites them to produce their own information sources.

> Identify all the legal terms in your source text and create a glossary with
> the definition of the term and possible equivalents, with their definitions,
> in the target legal culture. Do not use bilingual dictionaries and make
> sure you refer to monolingual dictionaries and other resources such as
> text books.

(c) Critical analysis

This exercise promotes reflection about the translation process by suggesting the analysis of a given source text and its translation. Trainees should not focus on spotting mistakes but they should instead highlight (appropriate) translation solutions and strategies.

> Analyse a source text of your choice and its target text. Reflect on the translation process that has taken place in order to produce the target text and comment on the translation brief, the role played by comparative law, the nature of the decisions taken, and the like.

11.4.4 Identification and recognition of translation problems: Culture-bound exercises

(a) False friends (Germany, England and Wales and Spain as source and target legal systems)

As happens in the case of standard lexis, the use of synonyms can also be considered a common practice in legal discourse, though, after closer consideration, exact synonyms tend to be very rare. Attention needs to be also paid to the fact that some legal terms can be dangerously misguiding in their apparent transparency or similarity to other familiar terms. It is advisable never to take unfamiliar legal terms at face value, especially when dealing with a foreign legal system.

> Consider the following terms:
>
> *Privatrecht/Zivilrecht/bürgerliches Recht*
> *Derecho privado/Derecho Civil*
> *Civil law*
>
> Are they synonyms? What is the difference between *bürgerliches Recht* and *Zivilrecht*? Which would be the best equivalent for the Spanish term *Derecho Civil*? And which for the English term *civil law*?

> Consider the following terms:
>
> *Schwurgericht/jurado/jury*
>
> Are they equivalent? Describe their similarities and differences in the three legal systems.

(b) Diachroneity (England and Wales and Ireland as source legal systems)

Except on very special occasions, lawyers would never use in their working practice legal texts that have been derogated by more recent ones, whilst translators may have to translate legal documents enacted under previous legislation. This implies that the meaning of some legal terms or realities may have changed from the time when the legislative disposition to which the document refers was in force and the moment when the document is translated. Given their inherent function to impose rights and duties, legal concepts automatically imply certain effects within a legal system and translators must therefore be conscious of the fact that choosing one term over another may lead to erroneous interpretation and create different legal effects.

> Find out the meaning of the following terms belonging to the English and Irish legal systems and suggest an equivalent in your target legal culture:
>
> – Divorce *a mensa et thoro*
> – Guardian *ad litem*
> – Anton Piller order
> – Mareva injunction

11.4.5 Comparison: General exercises

(a) Textology and terminology/phraseology

This exercise requires comparing two sets of documents belonging to two different legal cultures as far as textology and terminology/phraseology are concerned. Trainees are asked to produce one table comparing the main macro-structural elements and a second one contrasting the terminology and phraseology used in the documents to express the same realities. The aim of the macro-structural comparison is not only to make students reflect on how the same document can sometimes be found in different forms in a given culture, but also to make them aware of the divergent textual conventions in legal cultures. The terminology and phraseology analysis must not focus on offering translation solutions for a particular term or expression but rather on finding equivalent terms and expressions within the documents. Those equivalent terms and expressions will be useful later for translating documents, not necessarily for (just) the same text type as those used for the exercise. In addition to the macro-structural approach, the content can be also compared, as seen in Section 11.3, where permanent employment contracts between France and Spain have been compared.

> Create a corpus of documents on any legal aspect (for example, divorce decrees, sale contracts, birth or marriage certificates, etc.) belonging to two of the legal cultures you work with. From those corpora, create a table comparing the main macro-structural elements and another one comparing terminology and phraseology. Do not translate terms or expressions found in any corpus/document but offer equivalents found in both legal systems.

(b) Terminology

Following the methodology proposed by the Berlin *Internationales Institut für Rechts- und Verwaltungssprache* (see Section 11.2), the aim of this exercise is to dissect and analyse terms belonging to a particular legal aspect in two legal cultures in order to decide if they can be considered to be equivalent or not, or whether a partial equivalence exists.

> Select various texts that deal with the same legal aspect in two different legal cultures. Chose a series of terms in each of the cultures that could be *a priori* thought to be equivalent and used to translate one for another. Dissect the terms into essential and accidental characteristics and decide on their degree of equivalence.
>
> N.B.: Remember that, according to Cabré (1995), essential characteristics are those that define the essence of a term and cannot be avoided in the definition of the term, whilst accidental characteristics add elements irrelevant for the description (see Section 11.2.1).

(c) Terminology

The following exercise goes one step further and the objective is now to find translation solutions when no equivalent term has been found in the target language to translate a particular concept. Trainees can be offered a battery of translation techniques to choose from or, depending on their competence level, they may be asked to come up with their own strategies.

> From the terms discussed in the previous exercise, select those for which no equivalent term has been found and, using different translation techniques, offer a translation for those terms. If in the previous exercise an equivalent term has been found for all the terms, chose any other term/s in your source legal culture for which no equivalent term/s exist in your target legal culture.

11.4.6 Comparison: Culture-bound exercises

(a) Finding equivalents or applying different translation strategies (Italy as source legal culture)

Linguistic false friends can lead to misleading and inaccurate translations of legal terms and it is therefore vital to pay attention to the real meaning of the terms to avoid these pitfalls.

> With the help of monolingual dictionaries, explain the meaning of the terms listed below. Dissect the terms and try to find an equivalent in your target legal system. If you have not been able to find an equivalent, apply different translation techniques and explain why you have decided to go for them:
>
> *Notaio, cancelliere, avvocato, cassazionista, giudice istruttore, consulente tecnico d'ufficio, magistrato inquirente, magistrato giudicante.*

(b) Finding equivalents (France as source legal system)

Though primarily a comparative exercise, it also raises awareness of the asymmetries that exist between different legal systems and of the difficulty or even impossibility of finding an appropriate equivalent for a particular concept in the target legal culture.

> You have been asked to translate a leaflet about legal professionals in France that will be distributed in different languages at French embassies, consulates and other official institutions round the world. The terms to be translated are the following: *magistrat, magistrat du siège, magistrat du parquet, greffier, huissier de justice, procureur.*
>
> Create a list of the main characteristics of these professionals and the ones you would identify as equivalent in your target legal culture. Then decide, in each case, if it is possible to find an equivalent. When you have identified a possible equivalent, indicate if you would use it in the given communicative situation or if, on the contrary, other translation strategies could be more successfully used.

(c) Partial equivalence (Germany and Spain as target and source legal systems)

As stated before, some terms often have no exact equivalence in the legal system of the target language, but rather a partial equivalence. In such cases, it may be advisable to use a neutral or literal translation rather than a functional solution, as using a term which may also exist in the target system, albeit with a (somewhat) different meaning, might induce to error.

> According to the composition and jurisdiction of the following instances, find their similarities and differences:
>
> | | |
> |---|---|
> | *Juzgado de Primera Instancia e Instrucción* | *Amtsgericht* |
> | *Audiencia Provincial* | *Landgericht* |
> | *Tribunal Superior de Justicia* | *Oberlandesgericht* |

(d) Applying different translation strategies (France as source legal system)

This exercise is quite similar in nature to the previous one. However, in this case, the search for equivalent terms is not recommended as the institutions for which a translation is needed are strongly culturally bound to the source culture and if they were adapted to a different legal culture they could lead to misunderstandings.

> Suggest a translation for the following French courts in the language of your target legal system. Do not look for equivalent institutions but rather offer translation solutions using some of the translation techniques available to legal translators:
>
> *Conseil d'État, Cour de cassation, cour d'appel, cour d'assises, tribunal correctionnel, tribunal de police, tribunal de grande instance, tribunal d'instance, conseil de prud'hommes.*

Appendix 1

Contrat de travail à durée indéterminée – Salarié du Particulier employeur

Cesu
Un service des Urssaf

Contrat de travail
à durée indéterminée
Salarié du Particulier employeur

www.cesu.urssaf.fr

Entre l'employeur :

Mme, M.

Nom de naissance : .... Nom d'usage : ....

Prénom : .... Adresse : ....

....

Ville : .... Code postal : ....

N° de téléphone : .... N° Urssaf : .... Code NAF : 950Z.

Et le ou la salarié(e) :

Mme, M.

Nom de naissance : .... Nom d'usage : ....

Prénom : ....

Adresse : ....

....

Ville : ....

Code postal : .... N° de Sécurité sociale : ....

Les termes du contrat :

Il est conclu un contrat de travail régi par les dispositions de la Convention collective nationale (CCN) des salariés du particulier employeur.
La convention est tenue à la disposition du salarié qui pourra la consulter sur le lieu de travail.
Toute modification de ces textes lui sera notifiée dans le délai d'un mois après sa date d'effet.

Organismes de retraite et de prévoyance

Les institutions compétentes en matière de retraite et prévoyance sont :
IRCEM Retraite - 261, avenue des Nations Unies - 59 672 ROUBAIX CEDEX 1 - Tél. : 0980 980 990
IRCEM Prévoyance - 261, avenue des Nations Unies - 59 672 ROUBAIX CEDEX 1 - Tél. : 0980 980 990

Date d'entrée : . / / ..

Durée de la période d'essai : ....

(Renouvellement possible sous réserve d'information écrite avant la fin de la première période. Art. 8 CCN)

Lieu habituel de travail

Adresse : ....

....Ville : .... Code postal : ....

Autres lieux

Adresse : ....

....Ville : .... Code postal : ....

⑦ Nature de l'emploi (à cocher selon le cas)

Emplois ménagers et familiaux
- ☐ Employé de maison
- ☐ Employé familial

Postes d'emploi à caractère familial
- ☐ Assistant de vie
- ☐ Employé familial auprès d'enfants
- ☐ Dame ou homme de compagnie
- ☐ Garde-malade de jour à l'exclusion de soins
- ☐ Garde-malade de nuit à l'exclusion de soins
- ☐ Nurse
- ☐ Gouvernante d'enfant(s)

Emplois spécifiques
- ☐ Repasseuse familiale
- ☐ Homme et femme toutes mains
- ☐ Garde partagée : garde d'enfants au domicile de l'employeur
- ☐ Cuisinier qualifié
- ☐ Femme de chambre
- ☐ Valet de chambre
- ☐ Lingère
- ☐ Repasseuse qualifiée
- ☐ Secrétaire particulier
- ☐ Maître d'hôtel
- ☐ Chauffeur
- ☐ Chef cuisinier
- ☐ Secrétaire particulier bilingue

⑧ Description du poste : ....
....
....
....

⑨ Niveau de qualification

Niveau : .... de la Convention collective nationale des salariés du particulier employeur (art. 2 CCN).

⑩ Horaires de travail hebdomadaire

Emplois ménagers, familiaux et spécifiques

Nombre d'heures de travail effectif : .... heures / semaine réparties comme suit :

Jour	Lundi	Mardi	Mercredi	Jeudi	Vendredi	Samedi	Dimanche
Heure d'arrivée	.... h.......	.... h.......	.... h.......	.... h.......	.... h.......	.... h.......	.... h.......
Heure de départ	.... h.......	.... h.......	.... h.......	.... h.......	.... h.......	.... h.......	.... h.......
Durée travail effectif	.... h.......	.... h.......	.... h.......	.... h.......	.... h.......	.... h.......	.... h.......

Postes d'emploi à caractère familial

Nombre d'heures de travail effectif : .... heures / semaine réparties comme suit :

Jour	Lundi	Mardi	Mercredi	Jeudi	Vendredi	Samedi	Dimanche
Heure d'arrivée	.... h.......	.... h.......	.... h.......	.... h.......	.... h.......	.... h.......	.... h.......
Heure de départ	.... h.......	.... h.......	.... h.......	.... h.......	.... h.......	.... h.......	.... h.......
Durée présence réelle	.... h.......	.... h.......	.... h.......	.... h.......	.... h.......	.... h.......	.... h.......
Dont travail effectif	.... h.......	.... h.......	.... h.......	.... h.......	.... h.......	.... h.......	.... h.......
Et présence responsable	.... h.......	.... h.......	.... h.......	.... h.......	.... h.......	.... h.......	.... h.......

Nombre d'heures de présence responsable : .... heures correspondant à .... heures de travail effectif
(1 h de présence responsable = 2/3 d'1 h de travail effectif).

⑪ Jour de repos hebdomadaire : ....

Modalités particulières (s'il y a lieu) : ....

⊚ Jours fériés

Jours fériés travaillés : ☐ 1er janvier ☐ 8 mai ☐ 14 juillet ☐ 11 novembre
☐ Lundi de Pâques ☐ Jeudi de l'Ascension ☐ 15 août ☐ 25 décembre
☐ 1er mai ☐ Lundi de Pentecôte ☐ 1er novembre

⊚ Rémunération (art. 20 CCN)

Avec le Cesu déclaratif, le salaire net est majoré de **10 % au titre des congés payés.**

Salaire horaire brut (10% de congés payés inclus) avant déduction des cotisations sociales : €

Salaire horaire net (10% de congés payés inclus) après déduction des cotisations sociales : €

⊚ Indemnités kilométriques

Si le ou la salarié(e) utilise son véhicule : € / Km (art. 20-e CCN)

⊚ Prestations en nature

Nourriture : € / repas

Logement : € / mois

Les prestations en nature fournies seront déduites de la rémunération nette (art. 20-a 5 CCN).

⊚ Date de paiement de la rémunération : ....

⊚ Congés payes :

Délai de prévenance pour fixer les congés (l'article 16 de la CCN prévoit 2 mois minimum) : ....
Cas particulier de l'année d'embauche (année de référence incomplète).

⊚ Clauses particulières

- Congés liés aux contraintes professionnelles de l'employeur : ....
- Évolution possible des tâches, des horaires : ....
- Logement de fonction : ....
- Autres : ....

⊚ Le présent contrat est établi en deux exemplaires.

Signature de l'employeur
(précédée de « Lu et approuvé »)

Signature du salarié
(précédée de « Lu et approuvé »)

À.., le / /

À.., le / /

Modèle de contrat de travail issu de la Convention collective nationale des salariés du particulier employeur.

Appendix 2

Contrato de trabajo indefinido del servicio del hogar familiar

MINISTERIO
DE EMPLEO Y
SEGURIDAD SOCIAL

SERVICIO PÚBLICO
DE EMPLEO ESTATAL

CONTRATO DE TRABAJO INDEFINIDO DEL SERVICIO DE HOGAR FAMILIAR

CÓDIGO DE CONTRATO

DATOS DEL EMPLEADOR/A

| ☐ TIEMPO COMPLETO | 1 | 0 | 0 |
| ☐ TIEMPO PARCIAL | 2 | 0 | 0 |

| D./DÑA. | NIF./NIE | EN CONCEPTO (1) |

DATOS DE LA CUENTA DE COTIZACIÓN

| RÉGIMEN | COD. PROV. | NÚMERO | DIG. CONTR. |

DOMICILIO DE LA ACTIVIDAD

| C/ | MUNICIPIO | | C.P |

DATOS DEL/DE LA TRABAJADOR/A

| D./DÑA. | NIF./NIE (2) | FECHA DE NACIMIENTO |

| Nº AFILIACIÓN S.S. | NIVEL FORMATIVO | | NACIONALIDAD |

| MUNICIPIO DEL DOMICILIO | | PAÍS DOMICILIO |

Con la asistencia legal, en su caso, de D./Dña. ....
con NIF./NIE. ...., en calidad de (3) ....

DECLARAN

Que reúnen los requisitos exigidos para la celebración del presente contrato y, en su consecuencia, acuerdan formalizarlo con arreglo a las siguientes:

CLÁUSULAS

PRIMERA: El/la trabajador/a prestará sus servicios como (4) ...., en el domicilio de trabajo ubicado en (calle, nº y localidad) ....

SEGUNDA: La jornada de trabajo será:

☐ **A tiempo completo**: la jornada de trabajo será de .... horas semanales, prestadas de .... a ...., con los descansos establecidos legalmente.

☐ **A tiempo parcial**: la jornada de trabajo ordinaria será de ...., horas ☐ al día, ☐ a la semana, ☐ al mes, ☐ al año, siendo esta jornada inferior a la jornada máxima legal, que es de 40 horas semanales en cómputo anual.

Mod. PE-171A (I)

http://www.sepe.es

La distribución del tiempo de trabajo será de ....
....

TERCERA: SI ☐   NO ☐ , se acuerda la prestación de horas de presencia a disposición del empleador. Las horas de presencia serán ....horas semanales, distribuidas de la siguiente manera...
....El tiempo de presencia será objeto de retribución o compensación de la forma siguiente (5) :

☐ Compensación con períodos equivalentes de descanso retribuido.

☐ Retribución con un salario de cuantía no inferior al correspondiente a las horas ordinarias.

☐ De cualquiera de las anteriores maneras

CUARTA: La duración del presente contrato será INDEFINIDA, iniciándose la relación laboral en fecha .... y se establece un período de prueba de (6) ....

QUINTA: SI ☐   NO ☐ , se acuerda que el/la empleado/a de hogar pernocte en el domicilio del empleador.El régimen de las pernoctas será de ....
noches a la semana. Durante el descanso semanal y el periodo de vacaciones el/la trabajador/a no está obligado a residir en el domicilio del empleador.

SEXTA: El/la trabajador/a percibirá una retribución total de .... euros brutos (7) .... que se distribuirán en los siguientes conceptos salariales (8) ....

         SI ☐   NO ☐   ,se pactan retribuciones en especie (9). Las retribuciones en especie consistirán en :..................
....

SEPTIMA: La duración de las vacaciones anuales será de (10) ....

OCTAVA: Si la obligación de cotizar se ha iniciado a partir del 1 de enero de 2012, se aplicará una reducción del 20% a las cotizaciones devengadas. Esta reducción se ampliará con una bonificación hasta llegar al 45% en el caso de familias numerosas, si se cumplen los requisitos de la Ley 40/2003, de 18 de noviembre. ☐ (11)

NOVENA: En lo no previsto en este contrato, se estará a la legislación vigente que resulte de aplicación, y particularmente al Real Decreto 1620/2011, de 14 de noviembre, por el que se regula la relación laboral de carácter especial del servicio de hogar familiar y supletoriamente, en lo que resulte compatible, el Estatuto de los Trabajadores, aprobado por el R.D.Legislativo 1/1995, de 24 de marzo(BOE de 29 de marzo) excepto su artículo 33 que no se aplicará.

DÉCIMA: El contenido del presente contrato se presentará en la Tesorería General de la S. Social en el trámite de alta de el/la empleado/a de hogar en Seguridad Social a efectos de comunicación del contenido del contrato al Servicio Público de Empleo (12).

CLÁUSULAS ADICIONALES

Y para que conste, se extiende este contrato por triplicado ejemplar en el lugar y fecha a continuación indicados, firmando las partes interesadas.
En .... a .... de .... de 20 ....

El/la trabajador/a   El/la representante   El/la representante legal
                                         de la Empresa   del/de la menor, si procede

(1)	Titular en el Hogar.
(2)	En el caso de contratación a través de contingente a una persona extranjera no comunitaria y no residente en España, deberá cumplimentarse el anexo Mod. PE- 217
(3)	Padre, madre, tutor/a o persona o institución que le tenga a su cargo.
(4)	Indicar profesión.
(5)	Señálese lo que proceda.
(6)	Habrá de respetarse, en todo caso, lo dispuesto en el art. 14.1 del Estatuto de los Trabajadores, no pudiendo superar dos meses.
(7)	A la hora, al día, a la semana o al mes.
(8)	Si la retribución es en horas, el salario comprenderá la retribución global de la parte proporcional del descanso semanal, pagas extraordinarias y vacaciones..
(9)	Las retribuciones en especie no podrán ser superiores al 30% de las retribuciones totales del trabajador.Deberá garantizarse el pago en dinero de la cuantía del S.M.I. en cómputo mensual en proporción a la jornada.
(10)	Mínimo: 30 días naturales.
(11)	Marcar en caso de tener derecho a la bonificación por familia numerosa.
(12)	PROTECCIÓN DE DATOS.- Los datos consignados en el presente modelo tendrán la protección derivada de Ley Orgánica 15/1999, de 13 de diciembre (BOE de 14 de diciembre).

Mod PE-17/R(II)

Bibliography

Arminjon, P., B. Nolde and M. Wolff. 1950. *Traité de Droit Comparé. Legal Monographs and Treatises. Book 10.* <http://digitalcommons.law.scu.edu/monographs/10>, accessed 12 May 2016.

Atiyah, P. S. and R. S. Summers. 1991. *Form and Substance in Anglo-American Law: A Comparative Study of Legal Reasoning, Legal Theory, and Legal Institutions.* Oxford: Clarendon Press.

Bellodi Ansaloni, A. 2015. *Linee essenziali di storia della scienza giuridica.* Rimini: Maggioli.

Bermann, G. A., P. Glenn, K. Lane Scheppele, A. Shalakany, D. V. Snyder, and E. Zoller. 2011. 'Comparative law: Problems and prospects'. *American University International Law Review* 26(4): 935–68.

Biel, L. and J. Engberg (eds). 2013. *Research Models and Methods in Legal Translation. Linguistica Antverpiensia New Series* 12.

Black, H. C. 1991. *Black's Law Dictionary.* 6th edn. St Paul, MN: West Publishing Co.

Borja Albi, A. 2000. *El texto jurídico inglés y su traducción al español.* Barcelona: Ariel.

Brand, O. 2009. 'Language as a barrier to comparative law'. In F. Olsen, A. Lorz and D. Stein (eds) *Translation Issues in Language and Law.* (pp. 18–34). Basingstoke: Palgrave Macmillan.

Byrne, R. and J. P. McCutcheon. 1990. *The Irish Legal System.* 2nd edn. Dublin: Butterworth.

_____. 2009. *The Irish Legal System.* 4th edn. Dublin: Butterworth.

Cabré, T. 1993. *La terminología. Teoría, metodología, aplicaciones.* Barcelona: Antártida/Empúries. [Spanish translation of Catalan original by Carles Tebé].

Calvo Encinas, E. 2002. 'La influencia de la asimetría procesal en la traducción jurídica: procedimientos de separación y divorcio en Irlanda y España'. *Puentes* 2: 37–52.

Caminade, M. and A. Pym.1998. 'Translator-training institutions'. In M. Baker (ed.) *Routledge Encyclopedia of Translation Studies.* (pp. 280–5). London: Routledge.

Cao, D. 1996. 'Towards a model of translation proficiency'. *Target* 8(2), 325–40.

_____. 2007. *Translating Law.* Clevedon: Multilingual Matters.

Dadomo, C. and S. Farran. 1996. *The French Legal System.* London: Sweet and Maxwell.

Dalla, D. 2004. *Introduzione a un corso romanistico.* 4th edn. Torino: Giappichelli.

David, R. 1950. *Traité élémentaire de droit civil comparé.* Paris: Librairie Générale de Droit et de Jurisprudence.

____. 1972. *French Law: Its Structure, Sources and Methodology*. Louisiana State University Press.

David, R. and J. Brierley. 1985. *Major Legal Systems in the World Today*. 3rd edn. London: Stevens and Sons.

De Cruz, P. 2007. *Comparative Law in a Changing World*. London: Routledge-Cavendish.

Dorbeck-Jung, B. R. 1995. 'Comparative legislative studies. A book of sketches towards a map of law of the world? Sources of law and legislation'. In E. Attwooll and P. Comanducci (eds) *Proceedings of the 17th World Congress of the International Association for Philosophy of Law and Social Philosophy*. Vol. 3. (pp. 94–103). Bologne.

Dullion, V. 2015. 'Droit comparé pour traducteurs: de la théorie à la didactique de la traduction juridique'. *International Journal for the Semiotics of Law* 28(1), 91–106.

EMT expert group. 2009. *Competences for Professional Translators, Experts in Multilingual and Multimedia Communication*. Brussels. <http://ec.europa.eu/dgs/translation/programmes/emt/key_documents/emt_competences_translators_en.pdf>, accessed 12 May 2016.

Engberg, J. 2013. 'Comparative law for translation: the key to successful mediation between legal systems'. In A. Borja and F. Prieto (eds) *Legal Translation in Context. Professional Issues and Prospects*. (pp. 9–26). Oxford: Peter Lang.

Esmein, A. 1905. 'Le Droit comparé et l'enseignement du droit'. *Congrès International de Droit Comparé*, Procès-verbaux des séances et documents I, 445.

Farnsworth, E. A. 1987. *Introduction to the Legal System of the United States*. New York: Oceana.

Federal Judicial Center. N.D. *The U.S. Legal System: A Short Description*. <http://www.fjc.gov/public/pdf.nsf/lookup/U.S._Legal_System_English07.pdf/$file/U.S._Legal_System_English07.pdf>, accessed 12 May 2016.

Fernández, R. 1989. *Manual de Historia del Derecho Español I. Las Fuentes*. Madrid: Centro de Estudios Ramón Areces.

Franzoni de Moldavski, A. 1996. 'La equivalencia funcional en la traducción jurídica'. *Voces* 20, 2–13.

García Maynez, E. 1940. *Introducción al estudio del Derecho*. 1st edn. Mexico: Porrua.

____. 2002. *Introducción al estudio del Derecho*. 53rd edn. Mexico: Porrua.

Gémar, J. C. (ed.). 1982. *Langage du droit et traduction. Essais de jurilinguistique. The Language of the Law and translation. Essays on Jurilinguistics*. Montreal: Linguatech.

____. 1988. 'La traduction juridique: art ou technique d'interprétation?', *Meta* 33(2), 305–19.

Glanert, S. (ed.) 2014. *Comparative Law – Engaging Translation*. Oxford: Routledge.

_____. 2011. *De la traductibilité du droit*. Paris: Dalloz.

Goff, L. 1997. 'The Future of the Common Law'. *International and Comparative Law Quarterly* 46(4), 745–60.

González, J. and R. Wagenaar. 2003. *Tuning Educational Structures in Europe. Final Report. Phase One*. Bilbao: Universidad de Deusto. <http://www.unideusto.org/tuning>, accessed 12 May 2016.

Grossi, P. 2006. *L'ordine giuridico medievale*. 7th edn. Roma: Laterza.

_____. 2012. *Introduzione al Novecento giuridico*. 2nd edn. Roma: Laterza.

Gutteridge, H. 1949. *Comparative Law: An Introduction to the Comparative Method of Legal Study and Research*. Cambridge: CUP.

Harding, A. and E. Örücü (eds). 2002. *Comparative Law in the 21st Century*. The Hague: Kluwer Academic Publishers.

Harvey, M. 2000. *A Beginner's Course in Legal Translation: The Case of Culture-bound Terms*. <http://www.tradulex.com/Actes2000/harvey.pdf>, accessed 12 May 2016.

Hatim, B. and I. Mason. 1990. *Discourse and the Translator*. London: Longman.

Hendry, J. 2014. 'Legal comparison and the (im)possibility of legal translation'. In S. Glanert (ed.) *Comparative Law – Engaging Translation*. (pp. 87–101). London: Routledge.

Hickey, L. 1993. 'Equivalence certainly, but is it legal?' *Turjumán* 2(2), 65–76.

Hönig, H. G. and P. Kussmaul. 1982. *Strategie der Übersetzung, Ein Lehr- und Arbeitsbuch*. Tübingen: Gunter Narr.

House, J. 1977. *A Model for Translation Quality Assessment*. Tübingen: Gunter Narr.

Hug, W. 1932. 'The history of comparative law'. *Harvard Law Review* 45(6), 1027–70.

Jessnitzer, K. 1982. *Ein Handbuch für die Praxis der Dolmetscher, Übersetzer und ihrer Auftraggeber im Gerichts-, Beurkundungs- und Verwaltungsverfahren*. Cologne: Heynemann.

Kelly, D. 2005. *A Handbook for Translator Trainers*. Manchester: St. Jerome.

Lambert, E. 1905. 'Conception générale et définition de la science du droit comparé', *Procès-verbaux des séances et documents, Congrès International de droit comparé I*.

Lambertini, R. 2006. *Introduzione allo studio esegetico del diritto romano*. 3rd edn. Bologna: Clueb.

Lavoie, J. 2003. 'Faut-il être juriste ou traducteur pour traduire le droit?'. *Meta* 48(3), 393–401.

Mattila, H. 2006. *Comparative Legal Linguistics*. Aldershot: Ashgate.

Merino Blanco, E. 1996. *The Spanish Legal System*. London: Sweet and Maxwell.

Merryman, J. H. 1985. *The Civil Law Tradition: An Introduction to the Legal Systems of Western Europe and Latin America*. 2nd edn. Stanford: Polity Press.

Merryman, J. H., D. S. Clark and J. O. Haley. 1994. 'Introduction to comparative law'. In J. H. Merryman, D. S. Clark and J. O. Haley (eds) *The Civil Law Tradition: Europe, Latin America, and East Asia*. (pp. 1–2). Charlottesville, VA: Michie Comp.

Nord, C. 1991. *Text Analysis in Translation*. Amsterdam: Rodopi.

_____. 1997. *Translating as a Purposeful Activity. Functionalist Approaches Explained*. Manchester: St. Jerome.

Örücü, E. 2002. '*Unde venit, quo tendit* comparative law?'. In A. Harding and E. Örücü (eds) *Comparative Law in the 21st Century*. (pp. 1–17). The Hague: Kluwer Academic Publishers.

Örücü, E. and D. Nelken. 2007. *Comparative Law: A Handbook*. Oxford: Hart.

PACTE. 2000. 'Acquiring translation competence: "Hypotheses and methodological problems of a research project"'. In A. Beeby, D. Ensinger and M. Presas (eds) *Investigating Translation*. (pp. 99–106). Amsterdam: John Benjamins.

Padoa Schioppa, A. 2007. *Storia del diritto in Europa. Dal medioevo all'età contemporanea*. Bologna: Il mulino.

Pelage, J. 2001. *Elements de traductologie juridique. Application aux langues romanes*. Paris: n.p.

Piecychna, B. 2013. 'Legal translation competence in the light of translational hermeneutics'. *Studies in Logic, Grammar and Rhetoric* 34(47), 141–59.

Pizzorusso, A. 1987. *Curso de derecho comparado*. Barcelona: Ariel.

Pommer, S. E. 2008. 'Translation as intercultural transfer: the case of law'. *SKASE Journal of Translation and Interpretation* 3(1), 17–21.

Prieto Ramos, F. 2009. 'Interdisciplinariedad y ubicación macrotextual en traducción jurídica'. *Translation Journal* 13(4): 1–9.

_____. 2011. 'Developing legal translation competence: an integrative process-oriented approach. Comparative legilinguistics'. *International Journal for Legal Communication* 5, 7–21.

Reiss, K. and J. Vermeer. 1996. *Fundamentos para una teoría funcional de la traducción*. Madrid: Akal. [Spanish translation of German original by Sandra García Reina, Celia Martín de León and Heidrun Witte].

Rojas Ulloa, M. F. 2009. 'Importancia del derecho comparado en el siglo XXI'. *Sapere* 4 <http://www.derecho.usmp.edu.pe/instituto/revista/articulos/Articulo_de_Investigacion_Juridica.pdf>, accessed 12 May 2016.

Sacco, R. 1991. 'Legal formants: a dynamic approach to comparative law'. *The American Journal of Comparative Law* 39(1), 1–34.

Šarčević, S. 1994. 'Translation and the law: an interdisciplinary approach', in M. Snell-Hornby, F. Pöchhacker and K. Kaindl (eds) *Translation Studies, an Interdiscipline*. (pp. 301–7). Amsterdam: John Benjamins.

_____. 1997. *New Approach to Legal Translation*. Dordrecht: Kluwer Law International.

Šarčević, S. and C. Robertson. 2013. 'The work of lawyer-linguists in the EU institutions'. In A. Borja and F. Prieto (eds) *Legal Translation in Context. Professional Issues and Prospects*. (pp. 181–202). Oxford: Peter Lang.

Scarpa, F. and D. Orlando. 2014. 'What it takes to do it right. An integrative EMT-based model for legal translation competence'. Paper presented at the QUALETRA Final Conference held in KU Leuven on 16–17 October. <http://www.eulita.eu/sites/default/files/orlando_scarpa_whatittakes.pptx>, accessed 12 May 2016.

Simonnaes, I. 2013. 'Legal translation and "traditional" comparative law – Similarities and differences'. *Linguistica Antverpiensia New Series* 12, 147–60.

Slapper, G. and D. Kelly. 2010. *English Law*. London: Routledge-Cavendish.

Snell-Hornby, M. 1988. *Translation Studies. An Integrated Approach*. Amsterdam: Benjamins.

Sparer, M. 2002. 'Peut-on faire de la traduction juridique? Comment doit-on l'enseigner?', *Meta* 47(2), 265–78.

Soriano-Barabino, G. 2002a. *Estudio de derecho comparado entre España e Irlanda como fase previa a la traducción de un expediente de crisis matrimonial*. MA Dissertation. Granada: University of Granada.

_____. 2002b. 'Incongruencia terminológica y equivalencia funcional en traducción jurídica: la guarda de menores en España e Inglaterra y Gales'. *Puentes* 2: 53–60.

_____. 2005. *La traducción de expedientes de crisis matrimoniales entre España e Irlanda: un estudio jurídico-traductológico*. PhD Thesis. Granada: University of Granada.

_____. 2013. 'La competencia temática en la formación de traductores de textos jurídicos en la combinación lingüística francés/español'. *Estudios de Traducción* 3, 45–56.

Steiner, E. 2010. *French Law: A Comparative Approach*. Oxford: Oxford University Press.

Terral, F. 2002. *La Traduction juridique dans un contexte de pluralisme linguistique. Le cas du Règlement (CE) 40/94 sur la marque communautaire*. PhD Thesis. Barcelona: University Autónoma de Barcelona.

Vermeer, J. 1986. 'Übersetzen als kultureller Transfer'. In M. Snell-Hornby (ed.) *Übersetzungswissenschaft – eine Neuorientierung*. (pp. 30–53). Tübingen: Francke.

Wagner, E., S. Bech and J. M. Martínez. 2002. *Translating for the European Union Institutions*. Manchester: St. Jerome.

Wilss, W. 1996. *Knowledge and Skills in Translator Behaviour*. Amsterdam: John Benjamins.

Zhao, X. and D. Cao. 2013. 'Legal translation at the United Nations'. In A. Borja and F. Prieto (eds) *Legal Translation in Context. Professional Issues and Prospects*. (pp. 203–20). Oxford: Peter Lang.

Zweigert, K. and H. Kötz. 1998. *Introduction to Comparative Law*. 3rd edn. Oxford: Oxford University Press.

Web pages

Eighth French Conference on Constitutional Law <http://www.droitconstitutionnel. org/congresNancy/atelierN3.html#listecom3>, accessed 12 May 2016.
European Master's in Translation (EMT): Competences for professional translators, experts in multilingual and multimedia communication <http://ec.europa.eu/ dgs/translation/programmes/emt/key_documents/emt_competences_translat ors_en.pdf>, accessed 12 May 2016.
German legal texts <http://www.gesetze-im-internet.de>, accessed 12 May 2016.
Introduction to German law <http://www.internetratgeber-recht.de>, accessed 12 May 2016.
Irish Courts Service <http://www.courts.ie>, accessed 12 May 2016.
Translated legal texts <http://www.gesetze-im-internet.de/Teilliste_translations. html>, accessed 12 May 2016.

Notes on Contributors

GUADALUPE SORIANO-BARABINO is Senior Lecturer of Translation Studies at the University of Granada, Spain. She holds a PhD in Legal Translation, a degree (*Licenciatura*) in Law and a degree (*Licenciatura*) in Translation and Interpreting from the University of Granada, as well as a BA in Applied Languages from Thames Valley University, UK, and a degree (*Maîtrise*) in Applied Languages from the University of Provence, France. She has studied law in Spain, Ireland, the UK and France and has worked as a solicitor in the UK. She has taught at the Universities of Ulster, Salamanca and Granada and has been invited to deliver lectures on legal translation at a number of universities. She has extensive experience as a sworn translator and interpreter for English, French and Spanish. Her main research and teaching areas are in legal translation, a discipline that she has been teaching at undergraduate and postgraduate level for over ten years. She is a member of the AVANTI research group.

ANGELA CARPI is a Research Fellow at the University of Bologna, Italy, and the lead lecturer of the course of *Lingua Giuridica* (Legal Language) taught at the law school of the same university. She has been a visiting lecturer at the University of La Plata, Argentina. Her research concentrates on comparative studies and her main topics of study are law and language, Chinese law, EU-China cooperation, contract law and environmental law.

RAFAEL ADOLFO ZAMBRANA KUHN has been teaching translation from German into Spanish at the University of Granada, Spain, since 1990. He holds a degree in English Philology and a degree in Translation (German/ Spanish). He has translated many books and articles and has specialized in the translation of legal and economic texts since 1997. He is a member of the AVANTI research group.

Index

NEW TRENDS IN TRANSLATION STUDIES

In today's globalised society, translation and interpreting are gaining visibility and relevance as a means to foster communication and dialogue in increasingly multicultural and multilingual environments. Practised since time immemorial, both activities have become more complex and multifaceted in recent decades, intersecting with many other disciplines. *New Trends in Translation Studies* is an international series with the main objectives of promoting the scholarly study of translation and interpreting and of functioning as a forum for the translation and interpreting research community.

This series publishes research on subjects related to multimedia translation and interpreting, in their various social roles. It is primarily intended to engage with contemporary issues surrounding the new multidimensional environments in which translation is flourishing, such as audiovisual media, the internet and emerging new media and technologies. It sets out to reflect new trends in research and in the profession, to encourage flexible methodologies and to promote interdisciplinary research ranging from the theoretical to the practical and from the applied to the pedagogical.

New Trends in Translation Studies publishes translation- and interpreting-oriented books that present high-quality scholarship in an accessible, reader-friendly manner. The series embraces a wide range of publications – monographs, edited volumes, conference proceedings and translations of works in translation studies which do not exist in English. The editor, Professor Jorge Díaz Cintas, welcomes proposals from all those interested in being involved with the series. The working language of the series is English, although in exceptional circumstances works in other languages can be considered for publication. Proposals dealing with specialised translation, translation tools and technology, audiovisual translation and the field of accessibility to the media are particularly welcomed.